SUPERNATURAL
HORROR IN LITERATURE
& OTHER LITERARY ESSAYS

SUPERNATURAL HORROR IN LITERATURE
& OTHER LITERARY ESSAYS

H.P. LOVECRAFT

INTRODUCTION BY
DARRELL SCHWEITZER

WILDSIDE PRESS

**SUPERNATURAL HORROR
IN LITERATURE & OTHER ESSAYS**

For more information, contact:
www.wildsidepress.com

CONTENTS

INTRODUCTION
by Darrell Schweitzer

In his pioneering *Lovecraft: A Biography* (1975) L. Sprague de Camp says of Lovecraft's essay "Supernatural Horror in Literature" that, whatever its merits, it "is a compilation of the sort that any professor of English literature could do." The clear implication is that if only Lovecraft had not "wasted" his time on such efforts, he would have produced more stories.

More stories by Lovecraft would have been wonderful indeed, but otherwise, despite the considerable merits of his biography and with all due respect for his numerous other achievements, our old friend Sprague could not have been more wrong.

Time will always tell in these cases, and it is now clear, as Lovecraft is incorporated into the canon of American literature, being reprinted in Penguin Classics, Modern Library, and Library of America, that any major piece of writing by Lovecraft is important in its own right. A treatise on the writing of poetry by an obscure college professor circa 1845 would be of interest only to antiquarians, but essays like "The Rationale of Verse" or "The Philosophy of Composition" by Edgar Allan Poe are of considerably greater significance precisely because they are by Poe. So it is with "Supernatural Horror in Literature." When a giant of literature speaks, we should listen.

As mere "compilation," too, "Supernatural Horror in Literature" has proven itself to be one of the best surveys of the subject published in the 20th century. Occasionally he may seem effusive in his praise of an individual work. (Is *The Shadowy Thing* by H.B. Drake as good as Lovecraft says it is? Opinions are divided.) Yet, overall, his judgments have proven sound. Poe scholar T.O. Mabbott acknowledged the brilliance of the chapter on Poe, including its very significant insight into "The Fall of the House of Usher."

Lovecraft's mention of many authors and works has been sufficient to insure their survival. Herbert Gorman's *A Place Called Dagon*, for example, is reprinted today entirely because Lovecraft mentioned it. Although Lovecraft had been directed to the works of William Hope Hodgson by others, his discussion of them has considerably stimulated subsequent interest in that writer. Any number of authors are today remembered primarily for what Lovecraft said about them. Many more, of substantial merit and reputation, continue to gain readership because people read about them in Lovecraft's essay first, then seek out their works. This is even true of such figures as Lord Dunsany, Arthur Machen, and Algernon Blackwood, three of the four of Lovecraft's "modern masters," whom he regarded the titans of the form. As for the fourth "master," one suspects that M.R. James has managed a small but steady presence in English literature without Lovecraft's help, though certainly

Lovecraft's praise has not hurt.

On the crassest, most commercial level, publishers of reprint editions know to mine Lovecraft's essay for blurbs. If you can get a cover quote by H.P. Lovecraft on a book, people will pick it up. With the possible exception of Poe, Lovecraft is now more famous than any of the writers he discusses in detail.

Furthermore, an insight we can gain from S.T. Joshi's subsequent *H.P. Lovecraft: A Life*, which builds on the de Camp biography and goes considerably beyond it, is that writing "Supernatural Horror in Literature" was, for Lovecraft, anything but a waste of time. Lovecraft began it in 1925 at the request of his friend, W. Paul Cook (who published the first version in his amateur magazine *The Recluse* in 1927), toward the end of his New York "exile," which his marriage to Sonia Greene was not working out and he had come to loathe life away from his beloved Providence. Frank Belknap Long reported that Lovecraft was in a fairly disturbed state of mind at this time, in a xenophobic "rage" about the "foreigners" who jostled against him in the subways and even claiming to carry a bottle of poison with him, with which to commit suicide if things became too unbearable. I myself have heard Long repeat this. It was never clear if he had ever actually seen the bottle of poison. But in any case, an extensive program of reviewing and catching up on spectral literature, and writing such an essay could only have done Lovecraft a great deal of good. Lovecraft himself reported that its benefits included clarifying his thoughts on the subject preparatory to writing more weird fiction, which is surely an adequate answer to de Camp. If Lovecraft needed to go to such lengths as a "warm-up exercise" to get the fiction flowing again, so be it. Also, the reading he did opened Lovecraft up to new influences. Despite some sloppy claims that Robert W. Chambers's *The King in Yellow* was a seminal influence on the Cthulhu Mythos and Lovecraft's conception of the *Necronomicon*, it is clear that Lovecraft only discovered Chambers — along with William Hope Hodgson — in the course of research for this essay, both for the initial version in *The Recluse* and for a subsequent revision.

The greatest significance of "Supernatural Horror in Literature," however, is as a formulation and statement of Lovecraft's aesthetics of the weird tale. Here the essay is again closely analogous to Poe's "The Rationale of Verse" etc. One does not go to those writings to learn how to write poetry. One goes to them to learn what Poe thought about writing poetry. Literary theory is not science. When concocted by a professor, who is otherwise not a practitioner of literature, it is of, to coin a phrase, academic interest. But the Ernest Hemingway theory of the realistic novel will tell us a great deal about Hemingway, even as Poe on poetry will tell us about poetry at least as it applies to Poe. Lovecraft on weird fiction helps us understand Lovecraft and appreciate the degree of thought that went into his work.

The key passage is this as Joshi emphasizes in *Lovecraft: a Life*:

> The true weird tale is more than secret murder, bloody bones, or a sheeted form clanking chains according to rule. A certain atmosphere of breathless and unexplainable dread of outer, unknown forces must be present, and there must be a hint, expressed with seriousness and portentousness becoming its subject, of that most terrible con-

ception of the human brain — a malign and particular suspension or defeat of those fixed laws of Nature which are our only safeguard against the assaults of chaos and the dæmons of unplumbed space.

Despite the slightly florid rhetoric, the dæmons of unplumbed space notwithstanding, this is the core of Lovecraft's compelling vision, which, far more than any subtle characterization or clever plotting, has made him certainly a very long-lasting writer, and perhaps — as our descendants will know in a couple centuries — one of the immortals of literature. The learned Mr. Joshi has written numerous essays, even whole books on Lovecraft's thought and aesthetics, but the core of it all is in that one paragraph, particularly in the last few lines. Dæmons of unplumbed space, indeed. Lovecraft saw mankind's existence as a trivial and fleeting incident in the vast and meaningless cosmos. Homer, the Bible, Shakespeare — and Lovecraft — will all be dust in a million years, an eyeblink of time on a cosmic scale, and in remote galaxies which appear as tiny specks of light when viewed from our largest telescopes, nothing mankind has ever done will make the slightest difference, nor will any creatures living there have any way of knowing that we ever existed. But the same applies to those creatures too. In the Lovecraftian universe — which is the universe revealed by science — art, civilization, intelligence, and even organic life are minor, local affairs.

Lovecraft's whole philosophy was based on this realization. An active "God" was an absurdity in such a universe. Therefore, any meaning we get out of life, we must put into it. The driving force, for Lovecraft, is aesthetics, not morality in the sense of rules enforced by some deity. In literature, then, the chief subject is the confrontation with the unknown, and the imaginative leap into the depths of "unplumbed space." That is ultimately what Lovecraft was looking for in weird fiction. He was less interested in romantic or vengeful specters posthumously righting human wrongs. He was more interested in something like William Hope Hodgson's *The House on the Borderland* or Lord Dunsany's "unreverberate laughter of the abyss."

"Supernatural Horror," then, is hardly just a survey that a college professor could do. It is the keystone to the edifice of Lovecraft's art.

Appended to this edition are two short essays, "Notes on Writing Weird Fiction," which is a how-to article of the sort many writers produce, useful for elucidating Lovecraft's method of constructing a story, and again, restating some of his aesthetic ideas. It originally appeared in *The Amateur Correspondent* for May-June 1937 (i.e. shortly after Lovecraft's death).

"Some Notes on Interplanetary Fiction," published in *The Californian*, Winter 1935 (another amateur publication) is both an aesthetic statement and a ringing tirade against what Lovecraft saw as the sorry state of science fiction at the time. It is clear from his letters (particularly those to Willis Connover, as quoted in *Lovecraft at Last*) that Lovecraft was no particular fan of the science fiction pulp magazines of the middle '30s. He had not read E.E. "Doc" Smith's works, he told Connover, because adult correspondents whose judgment he trusted told him that Smith was on the level of a dime-novelist and of no serious merit. He does put in a good word for Stanley G. Weinbaum, but had otherwise given up on *Wonder Stories, Astounding Stories,* and *Amazing Stories* as "hopeless." This is, in retrospect, a defensible position from the perspective of 1935. There were a handful of Wellsian pastiches by John W. Campbell writing as Don A. Stuart in *Astounding,* but otherwise, the great bulk of the material in the main three science fiction pulps — not to mention frequent science fiction serials in *Argosy,* most of them by or inspired by Edgar Rice Burroughs — were pretty much as Lovecraft described them: formulaic, contrived, and completely implausible.

If Lovecraft had lived to a normal life-expectancy, rather than dying at age 46 and some months, he could well have made it into the 1960s. He would have witnessed the considerable maturation of science fiction beginning with John W. Campbell's editorship of *Astounding* from 1938 on. He would probably have appreciated Campbell's increased seriousness and insistence on scientific realism, but it's just as likely he would have been repelled by Campbell's jaunty "can-do" engineering optimism. His own insistence on scientific accuracy ("Everything must be in strict accord with the known or assumed nature of the orb in question — surface gravity, axial inclination . . .") suggests that he might have appreciated the works of Hal Clement on some level, though he probably would have found Clement, too, unconvincingly upbeat and cheerful. My own guess is that if Lovecraft had lived a normal lifespan, he would have continued publishing in *Weird Tales,* been largely unsuccessful in selling to John W. Campbell (though he might have gotten a tale or two into *Unknown,* Campbell's fantasy magazine, 1939-1943) and probably would have eked out a precarious existence in such secondary magazines as *Famous Fantastic Mysteries* (a decidedly old-fashioned publication, mostly devoted to reprints, including some Lovecraft, but also a source for some original fiction) until the advent of *The Magazine of Fantasy and Science Fiction* (beginning in 1949 as *The Magazine of Fantasy*), which he would have heralded as the first genuine attempt to produce a magazine of fantastic fiction to a real literary standard.

But of course none of that happened. Nor did "Some Notes on Interplanetary Fiction," being published where it was, in an amateur magazine which wasn't even distributed to science-fiction fans, have the sort of impact it should have, as a wake-up call to lazy writers. It, and "Notes on Writing Weird Fiction," did not become generally available until August Derleth reprinted them in the Arkham House volume *Marginalia* in 1944. However, "Some Notes on Interplanetary Fiction" is still of considerable interest, not merely because Lovecraft late in his career was moving in the direction of outright science fiction — his "At the Mountains of Madness" and "The Shadow Out of Time" has been submitted by others to *Astounding* and published there in 1936, where they proved an uneasy fit — but because a good deal of what he has to say is still true.

SUPERNATURAL HORROR
IN LITERATURE

I.

Introduction

THE oldest and strongest emotion of mankind is fear, and
the oldest and strongest kind of fear is fear of the unknown.
These facts few psychologists will dispute, and their admitted truth must establish for all time the genuineness and
dignity of the weirdly horrible tale as a literary form.
Against it are discharged all the shafts of a materialistic
sophistication which clings to frequently felt emotions and
external events, and of a naïvely insipid idealism which
deprecates the æsthetic motive and calls for a didactic literature to "uplift" the reader toward a suitable degree of smirk-
ing optimism. But in spite of all this opposition the weird
tale has survived, developed, and attained remarkable
heights of perfection; founded as it is on a profound and ele-
mentary principle whose appeal, if not always universal,
must necessarily be poignant and permanent to minds of
the requisite sensitiveness.

The appeal of the spectrally macabre is generally narrow because it demands from the reader a certain degree of imagination and a capacity for detachment from everyday life. Relatively few are free enough from the spell of the daily routine to respond to tappings from outside, and tales of ordinary feelings and events, or of common sentimental distortions of such feelings and events, will always take first place in the taste of the majority; rightly, perhaps, since of course these ordinary matters make up the greater part of human experience. But the sensitive are always with us, and sometimes a curious streak of fancy invades an obscure corner of the very hardest head; so that no amount of rationalisation, reform, or Freudian analysis can quite annul the thrill of the chimney-corner whisper or the lonely wood. There is here involved a psychological pattern or tradition as real and as deeply grounded in mental experience as any other pattern or tradition of mankind; coeval with the religious feeling and closely related to many aspects of it, and too much a part of our innermost biological heritage to lose keen potency over a very important, though not numerically great, minority of our species.

Man's first instincts and emotions formed his response to the environment in which he found himself. Definite feelings based on pleasure and pain grew up around the phenomena whose causes and effects he understood, whilst around those which he did not understand — and the universe teemed with them in the early days — were naturally woven such personifications, marvelous interpretations, and sensations of awe and fear as would be hit upon by a race having few and simple ideas and limited experience. The unknown, being likewise the unpredictable, became for our primitive forefathers a terrible and omnipotent source of boons and calamities visited upon mankind for cryptic and wholly extra-terrestrial reasons, and thus clearly belonging to spheres of existence whereof we know nothing and wherein we have no part. The phenomenon of dreaming likewise helped to build up the notion of an unreal or spiritual world; and in general, all the conditions of savage dawn — life so strongly conducted toward a feeling of the supernatural, that we need not wonder at the thoroughness with which man's very hereditary essence has become saturated with religion and superstition. That saturation must, as a matter of plain scientific fact, be regarded as virtually permanent so far as the subconscious mind and inner instincts are concerned; for though the area of the unknown has been steadily contracting for thousands of years, an infinite reservoir of mystery still engulfs most of the outer cosmos, whilst a vast residuum of powerful inherited associations clings round all the objects and processes that were once mysterious, however well they may now be explained. And more than this, there is an actual physiological fixation of the old instincts in our nervous tissue, which would make them obscurely operative even were the conscious mind to be purged of all sources of wonder.

Because we remember pain and the menace of death more vividly than pleasure, and because our feelings toward the beneficent aspects of the unknown have from the first been captured and formalised by conventional religious rituals, it has fallen to the lot of the darker and more maleficent side of cosmic mystery to figure chiefly in our popular supernatural folklore. This tendency, too, is naturally enhanced by the fact that uncertainty and danger are always closely allied; thus making any kind of an unknown world a world of peril and evil possibilities. When to this sense of fear and evil the inevitable fascination of wonder and curiosity is superadded, there is born a composite body of keen emotion and imaginative provocation whose vitality must of necessity endure as long as the human race itself. Children will always be afraid of the dark, and men with minds sensitive to hereditary impulse will always tremble at the thought of the hidden and fathomless worlds of strange life which may pulsate in the gulfs beyond the stars, or press hideously upon our own globe in unholy dimensions which only the dead and the moonstruck can glimpse.

With this foundation, no one need wonder at the existence of a literature of cosmic fear. It has always existed, and always will exist; and no better evidence of its tenacious vigour can be cited than the impulse which now and then drives writers of totally opposite leanings to try their hands at it in isolated tales, as if to discharge from their minds certain phantasmal shapes which would otherwise haunt them. Thus Dickens wrote several eerie narratives; Browning, the hideous poem *Childe Roland;* Henry James, *The Turn of the Screw;* Dr. Holmes, the subtle novel *Elsie Venner;* F. Marion Crawford, *The Upper Berth* and a number of other examples; Mrs. Charlotte Perkins Gilman, social worker, *The Yellow Wall Paper;* whilst the humorist, W. W. Jacobs, produced that able melodramatic bit called *The Monkey's Paw.*

This type of fear-literature must not be confounded with a type externally similar but psychologically widely different; the literature of mere physical fear and the mundanely gruesome. Such writing, to be sure, has its place, as has the conventional or even whimsical or humorous ghost story where formalism or the author's knowing wink removes the true sense of the morbidly unnatural; but these things are not the literature of cosmic fear in its purest sense. The true weird tale has something more than secret murder, bloody bones, or a sheeted form clanking chains according to rule. A certain atmosphere of breathless and unexplainable dread of outer, unknown forces must be present; and there must be a hint, expressed with a seriousness and portentousness becoming its subject, of that most terrible conception of the human brain — a malign and particular suspension or defeat of those fixed laws of Nature which are our only safeguard against the assaults of chaos and the dæmons of unplumbed space.

Naturally we cannot expect all weird tales to conform absolutely to any theoretical model. Creative minds are uneven, and the best of fabrics have their dull spots. Moreover, much of the choicest weird work is unconscious; appearing in memorable fragments scattered through material whose massed effect may be of a very different cast. Atmosphere is the all-important thing, for the final criterion of authenticity is not the dovetailing of a plot but the creation of a given sensation. We may say, as a general thing, that a weird story whose intent is to teach or produce a social effect, or one in which the horrors are finally explained away by natural means, is not a genuine tale of cosmic fear; but it remains a fact that such narratives often possess, in isolated sections, atmospheric touches which fulfill every condition of true supernatural horror-literature. Therefore we must judge a weird tale not by the author's intent, or by the mere mechanics of the plot; but by the emotional level which it attains at its least mundane point. If the proper sensations are excited, such a "high spot" must be admitted on its own merits as weird literature, no matter how prosaically it is later dragged down. The one test of the really weird is simply this — whether of not there be excited in the reader a profound sense of dread, and of contact with unknown spheres and powers; a subtle attitude of awed listening, as if for the beating of black wings or the scratching of outside shapes and entities on the known universe's utmost rim. And of course, the more completely and unifiedly a story conveys this atmosphere the better it is as a work of art in the given medium.

II.

The Dawn of the Horror Tale

As may naturally be expected of a form so closely connected with primal emotion, the horror-tale is as old as human thought and speech themselves.

Cosmic terror appears as an ingredient of the earliest folklore of all races, and is crystallised in the most archaic ballads, chronicles, and sacred writings. It was, indeed, a prominent feature of the elaborate ceremonial magic, with its rituals for the evocation of dæmons and spectres, which flourished from prehistoric times, and which reached its highest development in Egypt and the Semitic nations. Fragments like the Book of Enoch and the Claviculae of Solomon well illustrate the power of the weird over the ancient Eastern mind, and upon such things were based enduring systems and traditions whose echoes extend obscurely even to the present time. Touches of this transcendental fear are seen in classic literature, and there is evidence of its still greater emphasis in a ballad literature which paralleled the classic stream but vanished for lack of a written medium. The Middle Ages, steeped in fanciful darkness, gave it an enormous impulse toward expression; and East and West alike were busy preserving and amplifying the dark heritage, both of random folklore and of academically formulated magic and cabalism, which had descended to them. Witch, werewolf, vampire, and ghoul brooded ominously on the lips of bard and grandam, and needed but little encouragement to take the final step across the boundary that divides the chanted tale or song from the formal literary composition. In the Orient, the weird tale tended to assume a gorgeous colouring and sprightliness which almost transmuted it into sheer phantasy. In the West, where the mystical Teuton had come down from his black boreal forests and the Celt remembered strange sacrifices in Druidic groves, it assumed a terrible intensity and convincing seriousness of atmosphere which doubled the force of its half-told, half-hinted horrors.

Much of the power of Western horror-lore was undoubtedly due to the hidden but often suspected presence of a hideous cult of nocturnal worshippers whose strange customs — descended from pre-Aryan and pre-agricultural times when a squat race of Mongoloids roved over Europe with their flocks and herds — were rooted in the most revolting fertility-rites of immemorial antiquity. This secret religion, stealthily handed down amongst peasants for thousands of years despite the outward reign of the Druidic, Graeco-Roman, and Christian faiths in the regions involved, was marked by wild "Witches' Sabbaths" in lonely woods and atop distant hills on Walpurgis-Night and Hallowe'en, the traditional breeding-seasons of the goats and sheep and cattle; and became the source of vast riches of sorcery-legend, besides provoking extensive witchcraft-prosecutions of which the Salem affair forms the chief American example. Akin to it in essence, and perhaps connected with it in fact, was the frightful secret system of inverted theology or Satan-worship which produced such horrors as the famous "Black Mass"; whilst operating toward the same end we may note the activities of those whose aims were somewhat more scientific or philosophical — the astrologers, cabalists, and alchemists of the Albertus Magnus or Ramond Lully type, with whom such rude ages invariably abound. The prevalence and depth of the mediæval horror-spirit in Europe, intensified by the dark despair which waves of pestilence brought, may be fairly gauged by the grotesque carvings slyly introduced into much of the finest later Gothic ecclesiastical work of the time; the dæmoniac gar-goyles of Notre Dame and Mont St. Michel being among the most famous specimens. And throughout the period, it must be remembered, there existed amongst educated and uneducated alike a most unquestioning faith in every form of the supernatural; from the gentlest doctrines of Chris-tianity to the most monstrous morbidities of witchcraft and black magic. It was from no empty background that the Renaissance magicians and alchemists — Nostradamus, Tri-themius, Dr. John Dee, Robert Fludd, and the like — were born.

In this fertile soil were nourished types and characters of sombre myth and legend which persist in weird literature to this day, more or less disguised or altered by modern technique. Many of them were taken from the earliest oral sources, and form part of mankind's permanent heritage. The shade which appears and demands the burial of its bones, the dæmon lover who comes to bear away his still living bride, the death-fiend or psychopomp riding the night-wind, the man-wolf, the sealed chamber, the deathless sorcerer — all these may be found in that curious body of mediæval lore which the late Mr. Baring-Gould so effectively assembled in book form. Wherever the mystic Northern blood was strongest, the atmosphere of the popular tales became most intense; for in the Latin races there is a touch of basic rationality which denies to even their strangest superstitions many of the overtones of glamour so characteristic of our own forest-born and ice-fostered whisperings.

Just as all fiction first found extensive embodiment in poetry, so is it in poetry that we first encounter the permanent entry of the weird into standard literature. Most of the ancient instances, curiously enough, are in prose; as the werewolf incident in Petronius, the gruesome passages in Apuleius, the brief but celebrated letter of Pliny the Younger to Sura, and the odd compilation *On Wonderful Events* by the Emperor Hadrian's Greek freedman, Phlegon. It is in Phlegon that we first find that hideous tale of the corpsebride, *Philinnion and Machates*, later related by Proclus and in modern times forming the inspiration of Goethe's *Bride of Corinth* and Washington Irving's *German Student*. But by the time the old Northern myths take literary form, and in that later time when the weird appears as a steady element in the literature of the day, we find it mostly in metrical dress; as indeed we find the greater part of the strictly imaginative writing of the Middle Ages and Renaissance. The Scandinavian Eddas and Sagas thunder with cosmic horror, and shake with the stark fear of Ymir and his shapeless spawn; whilst our own Anglo-Saxon *Beowulf* and the later Continental Nibelung tales are full of eldritch weirdness. Dante is a pioneer in the classic capture of macabre atmosphere, and in Spenser's stately stanzas will be seen more than a few touches of fantastic terror in landscape, incident, and character. Prose literature gives us Malory's *Morte d'Arthur*, in which are presented many ghastly situations taken from early ballad sources — the theft of the sword and silk from the corpse in Chapel Perilous by Sir Galahad — whilst other and cruder specimens were doubtless set forth in the cheap and sensational "chapbooks" vulgarly hawked about and devoured by the ignorant. In Elizabethan drama, with its *Dr. Faustus,* the witches in *Macbeth,* the ghost in *Hamlet,* and the horrible gruesomeness of Webster we may easily discern the strong hold of the dæmoniac on the public mind; a hold intensified by the very real fear of living witchcraft, whose terrors, wildest at first on the Continent, begin to echo loudly in English ears as the witch-hunting crusades of James the First gain headway. To the lurking mystical prose of the ages is added a long line of treatises on witchcraft and dæmonology which aid in exciting the imagination of the reading world.

Through the seventeenth and into the eighteenth century we behold a growing mass of fugitive legendry and balladry of darksome cast; still, however, held down beneath the surface of polite and accepted literature. Chapbooks of horror and weirdness multiplied, and we glimpse the eager interest of the people through fragments like

Defoe's *Apparition of Mrs. Veal,* a homely tale of a dead woman's spectral visit to a distant friend, written to advertise covertly a badly selling theological disquisition on death. The upper orders of society were now losing faith in the supernatural, and indulging in a period of classic rationalism. Then, beginning with the translations of Eastern tales in Queen Anne's reign and taking definite form toward the middle of the century, comes the revival of romantic feeling — the era of new joy in nature, and in the radiance of past times, strange scenes, bold deeds, and incredible marvels. We feel it first in the poets, whose utterances take on new qualities of wonder, strangeness, and shuddering. And finally, after the timid appearance of a few weird scenes in the novels of the day — such as Smollett's *Adventures of Ferdinand, Count Fathom* — the release instinct precipitates itself in the birth of a new school of writing; the "Gothic" school of horrible and fantastic prose fiction, long and short, whose literary posterity is destined to become so numerous, and in many cases so resplendent in artistic merit. It is, when one reflects upon it, genuinely remarkable that weird narration as a fixed and academically recognized literary form should have been so late of final birth. The impulse and atmosphere are as old as man, but the typical weird tale of standard literature is a child of the eighteenth century.

III.

The Early Gothic Novel

THE shadow-haunted landscapes of Ossian, the chaotic visions of William Blake, the grotesque witch dances in

Burns's *Tam O'Shanter,* the sinister dæmonism of Coleridge's *Christobel* and *Ancient Mariner,* the ghostly charm of James Hogg's *Kilmeny,* and the more restrained approaches to cosmic horror in *Lamia* and many of Keats's other poems, are typical British illustrations of the advent of the weird to formal literature. Our Teutonic cousins of the Continent were equally receptive to the rising flood, and Burger's *Wild Huntsman* and the even more famous dæmon-bridegroom ballad of *Lenore* — both imitated in English by Scott, whose respect for the supernatural was always great — are only a taste of the eerie wealth which German song had commenced to provide. Thomas Moore adapted from such sources the legend of the ghoulish statue-bride (later used by Prosper Mérimée in *The Venus of Ille,* and traceable back to great antiquity) which echoes so shiveringly in his ballad of *The Ring;* whilst Goethe's deathless masterpiece *Faust,* crossing from mere balladry into the classic, cosmic tragedy of the ages, may be held as the ultimate height to which this German poetic impulse arose.

But it remained for a very sprightly and worldly Englishman — none other than Horace Walpole himself — to give the growing impulse definite shape and become the actual founder of the literary horror-story as a permanent form. Fond of mediæval romance and mystery as a dilettante's diversion, and with a quaintly imitated Gothic castle as his abode at Strawberry Hill, Walpole in 1764 published *The Castle of Otranto;* a tale of the supernatural which, though thoroughly unconvincing and mediocre in itself, was destined to exert an almost unparalleled influence on the literature of the weird. First venturing it only as a "translation" by one "William Marshal, Gent." from the Italian of a

mythical "Onuphrio Muralto," the author later acknowledged his connection with the book and took pleasure in its
wide and instantaneous popularity — a popularity which
extended to many editions, early dramatization, and whole-
sale imitation both in England and in Germany.

The story — tedious, artificial, and melodramatic — is
further impaired by a brisk and prosaic style whose urbane
sprightliness nowhere permits the creation of a truly weird
atmosphere. It tells of Manfred, an unscrupulous and
usurping prince determined to found a line, who after the
mysterious sudden death of his only son Conrad on the latter's bridal morn, attempts to put away his wife Hippolita
and wed the lady destined for the unfortunate youth — the
lad, by the way, having been crushed by the preternatural
fall of a gigantic helmet in the castle courtyard. Isabella, the
widowed bride, flees from his design; and encounters in
subterranean crypts beneath the castle a noble young pre-
server, Theodore, who seems to be a peasant yet strangely
resembles the old lord Alfonso who ruled the domain before
Manfred's time. Shortly thereafter supernatural phenomena
assail the castle in diverse ways; fragments of gigantic ar-
mour being discovered here and there, a portrait walking
out of its frame, a thunderclap destroying the edifice, and a
colossal armoured spectre of Alfonso rising out of the ruins
to ascend through parting clouds to the bosom of St. Nich-
olas. Theodore, having wooed Manfred's daughter Matilda
and lost her through death — for she is slain by her father by
mistake — is discovered to be the son of Alfonso and right-
ful heir to the estate. He concludes the tale by wedding
Isabella and preparing to live happily ever after, whilst
Manfred — whose usurpation was the cause of his son's

supernatural death and his own supernatural harassings —
retires to a monastery for penitence; his saddened wife
seeking asylum in a neighbouring convent.

Such is the tale; flat stilted, and altogther devoid of the
true cosmic horror which makes weird literature. Yet such
was the thirst of the age for those touches of strangeness and
spectral antiquity which it reflects, that it was seriously
received by the soundest readers and raised in spite of its
intrinsic ineptness to a pedestal of lofty importance in literary history. What it did above all else was to create a novel
type of scene, puppet-characters, and incidents; which, handled to better advantage by writers more naturally adapted
to weird creation, stimulated the growth of an imitative
Gothic school which in turn inspired the real weavers of
cosmic terror — the line of actual artists beginning with Poe.
This novel dramatic paraphernalia consisted first of all of
the Gothic castle, with its awesome antiquity, vast distances
and rambling, deserted or ruined wings, damp corridors,
unwholesome hidden catacombs, and galaxy of ghosts and
appalling legends, as a nucleus of suspense and dæmoniac
fright. In addition, it included the tyrannical and malevolent
nobleman as villain; the saintly, long-persecuted, and generally insipid heroine who undergoes the major terrors and
serves as a point of view and focus for the reader's sympa-
thies; the valorous and immaculate hero, always of high
birth but often in humble disguise; the convention of high-
sounding foreign names, mostly Italian, for the characters;
and the infinite array of stage properties which includes
strange lights, damp trap-doors, extinguished lamps,
mouldy hidden manuscripts, creaking hinges, shaking
arras, and the like. All this paraphernalia reappears with

amusing sameness, yet sometimes with tremendous effect, throughout the history of the Gothic novel; and is by no means extinct even today, though subtler technique now forces it to assume a less naïve and obvious form. An harmonious milieu for a new school had been found, and the writing world was not slow to grasp the opportunity.

German romance at once responded to the Walpole influence, and soon became a byword for the weird and ghastly. In England one of the first imitators was the celebrated Mrs. Barbauld, then Miss Aikin, who in 1773 published an unfinished fragment called *Sir Bertrand*, in which the strings of genuine terror were truly touched with no clumsy hand. A nobleman on a dark and lonely moor, attracted by a tolling bell and distant light, enters a strange and ancient turreted castle whose doors open and close and whose bluish will-o'-the-wisps lead up mysterious staircases toward dead hands and animated black statues. A coffin with a dead lady, whom Sir Bertrand kisses, is finally reached; and upon the kiss the scene dissolves to give place to a splendid apartment where the lady, restored to life, holds a banquet in honor of her rescuer. Walpole admired this tale, though he accorded less respect to an even more prominent offspring of his *Otranto* — *The Old English Baron*, by Clara Reeve, published in 1777. Truly enough, this tale lacks the real vibration to the note of outer darkness and mystery which distinguishes Mrs. Barbauld's fragment; and though less crude than Walpole's novel, and more artistically economical of horror in its possession of only one spectral figure, it is nevertheless too definitely insipid for greatness. Here again we have the virtuous heir to the castle disguised as a peasant and restored to his heritage through the ghost of his father; and here again we have a case of wide popularity leading to many editions, dramatization, and ultimate translation into French. Miss Reeve wrote another weird novel, unfortunately unpublished and lost.

The Gothic novel was now settled as a literary form, and instances multiply bewilderingly as the eighteenth century draws toward its close. *The Recess*, written in 1785 by Mrs. Sophia Lee, has the historic element, revolving round the twin daughters of Mary, Queen of Scots; and though devoid of the supernatural, employs the Walpole scenery and mechanism with great dexterity. Five years later, and all existing lamps are paled by the rising of a fresh luminary order — Mrs. Ann Radcliffe (1764-1823), whose famous novels made terror and suspense a fashion, and who set new and higher standards in the domain of macabre and fear-inspiring atmosphere despite a provoking custom of destroying her own phantoms at the last through labored mechanical explanations. To the familiar Gothic trappings of her predecessors Mrs. Radcliffe added a genuine sense of the unearthly in scene and incident which closely approached genius; every touch of setting and action contributing artistically to the impression of illimitable frightfulness which she wished to convey. A few sinister details like a track of blood on castle stairs, a groan from a distant vault, or a weird song in a nocturnal forest can with her conjure up the most powerful images of imminent horror; surpassing by far the extravagant and toilsome elaborations of others. Nor are these images in themselves any the less potent because they are explained away before the end of the novel. Mrs. Radcliffe's visual imagination was very strong, and appears as much in her delightful landscape touches — always in broad, glamorously pictorial outline, and never in close detail — as in her weird phantasies. Her prime weaknesses, aside from the habit of prosaic disillusionment, are a tendency toward erroneous geography and history and a fatal predilection for bestrewing her novels with insipid little poems, attributed to one or another of the characters.

Mrs. Radcliffe wrote six novels: *The Castles of Athlin and Dunbayne* (1789), *A Sicilian Romance* (1790), *The Romance of the Forest* (1792), *The Mysteries of Udolpho* (1794), *The Italian* (1797), and *Gaston de Blondeville*, composed in 1802 but first published posthumously in 1826. Of these *Udolpho* is by far the most famous, and may be taken as a type of the early Gothic tale at its best. It is the chronicle of Emily, a young Frenchwoman transplanted to an ancient and portentous castle in the Apennines through the death of her parents and the marriage of her aunt to the lord of the castle — the scheming nobleman, Montoni. Mysterious sounds, opened doors, frightful legends, and a nameless horror in a niche behind a black veil all operate in quick succession to unnerve the heroine and her faithful attendant, Annette; but finally, after the death of her aunt, she escapes with the aid of a fellow-prisoner whom she has discovered. On the way home she stops at a chateau filled with fresh horrors — the abandoned wing where the departed chatelaine dwelt, and the bed of death with the black pall — but is finally restored to security and happiness with her lover Valancourt, after the clearing-up of a secret which seemed for a time to involve her birth in mystery. Clearly, this is only familiar material re-worked; but it is so well re-worked that *Udolpho* will always be a classic. Mrs. Radcliffe's characters are puppets, but they are less markedly so than those of her forerunners. And in atmospheric creation she stands preëminent among those of her time.

Of Mrs. Radcliffe's countless imitators, the American novelist Charles Brockden Brown stands the closest in spirit and method. Like her, he injured his creations by natural explanations; but also like her, he had an uncanny atmospheric power which gives his horrors a frightful vitality as long as they remain unexplained. He differed from her in contemptuously discarding the external Gothic paraphernalia and properties and choosing modern American scenes for his Mysteries; but this repudiation did not extend to the Gothic spirit and type of incident. Brown's novels involve some memorably frightful scenes, and excel even Mrs. Radcliffe's in describing the operations of the perturbed mind. *Edgar Huntly* starts with a sleep-walker digging a grave, but is later impaired by touches of Godwinian didacticism. *Ormond* involves a member of a sinister secret brotherhood. That and *Arthur Mervyn* both describe the plague of yellow fever, which the author had witnessed in Philadelphia and New York. But Brown's most famous book is *Wieland; or, the Transformation* (1798), in which a Pennsylvania German, engulfed by a wave of religious fanaticism, hears "voices" and slays his wife and children as a sacrifice. His sister Clara, who tells the story, narrowly escapes. The scene, laid at the woodland estate of Mittingen on the Schuylkill's remote reaches, is drawn with extreme vividness; and the terrors of Clara, beset by spectral tones, gathering fears, and the sound of strange footsteps in the lonely house, are all shaped with truly artistic force. In the end a lame ventriloquial explanation is offered, but the atmosphere is genuine while it lasts. Carwin, the malign ventriloquist, is a typical villain of the Manfred or Montoni type.

IV.

The Apex of Gothic Romance

HORROR in literature attains a new malignity in the work of Matthew Gregory Lewis (1773-1818), whose novel *The Monk* (1796) achieved marvelous popularity and earned him the nickname "Monk" Lewis. This young author, educated in Germany and saturated with a body of wild Teuton lore unknown to Mrs. Radcliffe, turned to terror in forms more violent than his gentle predecessor had ever dared to think of; and produced as a result a masterpiece of active nightmare whose general Gothic cast is spiced with added stores of ghoulishness. The story is one of a Spanish monk, Ambrosio, who from a state of over-proud virtue is tempted to the very nadir of evil by a fiend in the guise of the maiden Matilda; and who is finally, when awaiting death at the Inquisition's hands, induced to purchase escape at the price of his soul from the Devil, because he deems both body and soul already lost. Forthwith the mocking Fiend snatches him to a lonely place, tells him he has sold his soul in vain since both pardon and a chance for salvation were approaching at the moment of his hideous bargain, and completes the sardonic betrayal by rebuking him for his unnatural crimes, and casting his body down a precipice whilst his soul is borne off for ever to perdition. The novel contains some appalling descriptions such as the incantation in the vaults beneath the convent cemetery, the burning of the convent, and the final end of the wretched abbot. In the sub-plot where the Marquis de las Cisternas meets the spectre of his erring ancestress, The Bleeding Nun, there are many enormously potent strokes; notably the visit of the animated corpse to the Marquis's bedside, and the cabalistic ritual whereby the Wandering Jew helps him to fathom and banish his dead tormentor. Nevertheless *The Monk* drags sadly when read as a whole. It is too long and too diffuse, and much of its potency is marred by flippancy and by an awkwardly excessive reaction against those canons of decorum which Lewis at first despised as prudish. One great thing may be said of the author: that he never ruined his ghostly visions with a natural explanation. He succeeded in breaking up the Radcliffian tradition and expanding the field of the Gothic novel. Lewis wrote much more than *The Monk*. His drama, *The Castle Spectre,* was produced in 1798, and he later found time to pen other fictions in ballad form — *Tales of Terror* (1799), *The Tales of Wonder* (1801), and a succession of translations from the German. Gothic romances, both English and German, now appeared in multitudinous and mediocre profusion. Most of them were merely ridiculous in the light of mature taste, and Miss Austen's famous satire *Northanger Abbey* was by no means an unmerited rebuke to a school which had sunk far toward absurdity. This particular school was petering out, but before its final subordination there arose its last and greatest figure in the person of Charles Robert Maturin (1782-1824), an obscure and eccentric Irish clergyman. Out of an ample body of miscellaneous writing which includes one confused Radcliffian imitation called *The Fatal Revenge; or, the Family of Montorio* (1807), Maturin at length envolved the vivid horror-masterpiece of *Melmoth, the Wanderer* (1820), in which the Gothic tale climbed to altitudes of sheer spiritual fright which it had never known before.

Melmoth is the tale of an Irish Gentleman who, in the seventeenth century, obtained a preternaturally extended life from the Devil at the price of his soul. If he can persuade another to take the bargain off his hands, and assume his existing state, he can be saved; but this he can never manage to effect, no matter how assiduously he haunts those whom despair has made reckless and frantic. The framework of the story is very clumsy; involving tedious length, digressive episodes, narratives within narratives, and labored dovetailing and coincidence; but at various points in the endless rambling there is felt a pulse of power undiscoverable in any previous work of this kind — a kinship to the essential truth of human nature, an understanding of the profoundest sources of actual cosmic fear, and a white heat of sympathetic passion on the writer's part which makes the book a true document of æsthetic self-expression rather than a mere clever compound of artifice. No unbiased reader can doubt that with *Melmoth* an enormous stride in the evolution of the horror-tale is represented. Fear is taken out of the realm of the conventional and exalted into a hideous cloud over mankind's very destiny. Maturin's shudders, the work of one capable of shuddering himself, are of the sort that convince. Mrs. Radcliffe and Lewis are fair game for the parodist, but it would be difficult to find a false note in the feverishly intensified action and high atmospheric tension of the Irishman whose less sophisticated emotions and strain of Celtic mysticism gave him the finest possible natural equipment for his task. Without a doubt Maturin is a man of authentic genius, and he was so recognized by

Balzac, who grouped *Melmoth* with Molière's *Don Juan*, Gœthe's *Faust,* and Byron's *Manfred* as the supreme allegorical figures of modern European literature, and wrote a whimsical piece called *Melmoth Reconciled,* in which the Wanderer succeeds in passing his infernal bargain on to a Parisian bank defaulter, who in turn hands it along a chain of victims until a reveling gambler dies with it in his possession, and by his damnation ends the curse. Scott, Rossetti, Thackeray and Baudelaire are the other titans who gave Maturin their unqualified admiration, and there is much significance in the fact that Oscar Wilde, after his disgrace and exile, chose for his last days in Paris the assumed name of "Sebastian Melmoth."

Melmoth contains scenes which even now have not lost their power to evoke dread. It begins with a deathbed — an old miser is dying of sheer fright because of something he has seen, coupled with a manuscript he has read and a family portrait which hangs in an obscure closet of his centuried home in County Wicklow. He sends to Trinity College, Dublin, for his nephew John; and the latter upon arriving notes many uncanny things. The eyes of the portrait in the closet glow horribly, and twice a figure strangely resembling the portrait appears momentarily at the door. Dread hangs over that house of the Melmoths, one of whose ancestors, "J. Melmoth, 1646," the portrait represents. The dying miser declares that this man — at a date slightly before 1800 — is alive. Finally the miser dies, and the nephew is told in the will to destroy both the portrait and a manuscript to be found in a certain drawer. Reading the manuscript, which was written late in the seventeenth century by an Englishman named Stanton, young John learns of a terrible incident in Spain in 1677, when the writer met a horrible fellow-countryman and was told of how he had stared to death a priest who tried to denounce him as one filled with fearsome evil. Later, after meeting the man again in London, Stanton is cast into a madhouse and visited by the stranger, whose approach is heralded by spectral music and whose eyes have a more than mortal glare. Melmoth the Wanderer — for such is the malign visitor — offers the captive freedom if he will take over his bargain with the Devil; but like all others whom Melmoth has approached, Stanton is proof against temptation. Melmoth's description of the horrors of a life in a madhouse, used to tempt Stanton, is one of the most potent passages of the book. Stanton is at length liberated, and spends the rest of his life tracking down Melmoth, whose family and ancestral abode he discovers. With the family he leaves the manuscript, which by young John's time is badly ruinous and fragmentary. John destroys both portrait and manuscript, but in sleep is visited by his horrible ancestor, who leaves a black and blue mark on his wrist.

Young John soon afterward receives as a visitor a shipwrecked Spaniard, Alonzo de Moncada, who has escaped from compulsory monasticism and from the perils of the Inquisition. He has suffered horribly — and the descriptions of his experiences under torment and in the vaults through which he once essays escape are classic — but had the strength to resist Melmoth the Wanderer when approached at his darkest hour in prison. At the house of a Jew who sheltered him after his escape he discovers a wealth of manuscript relating other exploits of Melmoth, including his wooing of an Indian island maiden, Immalee, who later comes into her birthright in Spain and is known as Donna Isidora; and of his horrible marriage to her by the corpse of a dead anchorite at midnight in the ruined chapel of a shunned and abhorred monastery. Moncada's narrative to young John takes up the bulk of Maturin's four-volume book; this disproportion being considered one of the chief technical faults of the composition.

At last the colloquies of John and Moncada are interrupted by the entrance of Melmoth the Wanderer himself, his piercing eyes now fading, and decrepitude swiftly overtaking him. The term of his bargain has approached its end, and he has come home after a century and a half to meet his fate. Warning all others from the room, no matter what sounds they may hear in the night, he awaits the end alone. Young John and Moncada hear frightful ululations, but do not intrude till silence comes toward morning. They then find the room empty. Clayey footprints lead out a rear door to a cliff overlooking the sea, and near the edge of the precipice is a track indicating the forcible dragging of some heavy body. The Wanderer's scarf is found on a crag some distance below the brink, but nothing further is ever seen or heard of him.

Such is the story, and none can fail to notice the difference between this modulated, suggestive, and artistically moulded horror and — to use the words of Professor George Saintsbury — "the artful but rather jejune rationalism of Mrs. Radcliffe, and the too often puerile extravagance, the bad taste, and the sometimes slipshod style of Lewis." Maturin's style in itself deserves particular praise, for its forcible directness and vitality lift it altogether above the pompous artificialities of which his predecessors are guilty. Professor Edith Birkhead, in her history of the Gothic novel, justly observes that "with all his faults Maturin was the greatest as well as the last of the Goths." *Melmoth* was widely read and eventually dramatized, but its late date in the evolution of the Gothic tale deprived it of the tumultuous popularity of *Udolpho* and *The Monk*.

V.

The Aftermath of Gothic Fiction

MEANWHILE other hands had not been idle, so that above the dreary plethora of trash like Marquis von Grosse's *Horrid Mysteries* (1796), Mrs. Roche's *Children of the Abbey* (1798), Mrs. Dacre's *Zofloya; or, the Moor* (1806), and the poet Shelley's schoolboy effusions *Zastro* (1810) and *St. Irvine* (1811) (both imitations of *Zofloya*) there arose many memorable weird works both in English and German. Classic in merit, and markedly different from its fellows because of its foundation in the Oriental tale rather than the Walpolesque Gothic novel, is the celebrated *History of the Caliph Vathek* by the wealthy dilettante William Beckford, first written in the French language but published in an English translation before the appearance of the original. Eastern tales, introduced to European literature early in the eighteenth century through Galland's French translation of the inexhaustibly opulent *Arabian Nights,* had become a reigning fashion; being used both for allegory and for amusement. The sly humour which only the Eastern mind knows how to mix with weirdness had captivated a sophisticated generation, till Bagdad and Damascus names became as freely strewn through popular literature as dashing Italian and Spanish ones were soon to be. Beckford, well read in Eastern romance, caught the atmosphere with unusual receptivity; and in his fantastic volume reflected very potently the haughty luxury, sly disillusion, bland cruelty, urbane treachery, and shadowy spectral horror of the Saracen spirit. His seasoning of the ridiculous seldom mars the force of his sinister theme, and the tale marches onward with a phantasmagoric pomp in which the laughter is that of skeletons feasting under arabesque domes. *Vathek* is a tale of the grandson of the Caliph Haroun, who, tormented by that ambition for super-terrestrial power, pleasure and learning which animates the average Gothic villain or Byronic hero (essentially cognate types), is lured by an evil genius to seek the subterranean throne of the mighty and fabulous pre-Adamite sultans in the fiery halls of Eblis, the Mahometan Devil. The descriptions of Vathek's palaces and diversions, of his scheming sorceress-mother Carathis and her witch-tower with the fifty one-eyed negresses, of his pilgrimage to the haunted ruins of Istakhar (Persepolis) and of the impish bride Nouronihar whom he treacherously acquired on the way, of Istakhar's primordial towers and terraces in the burning moonlight of the waste, and of the terrible Cyclopean halls of Eblis, where, lured by glittering promises, each victim is compelled to wander in anguish for ever, his right hand upon his blazingly ignited and eternally burning heart, are triumphs of weird colouring which raise the book to a permanent place in English letters. No less notable are the three *Episodes of Vathek*, intended for insertion in the tale as narratives of Vathek's fellow-victims in Eblis' infernal halls, which remained unpublished throughout the author's lifetime and were discovered as recently as

1909 by the scholar Lewis Melville whilst collecting material for his *Life and Letters of William Beckford*. Beckford, however, lacks the essential mysticism which marks the acutest form of the weird; so that his tales have a certain knowing Latin hardness and clearness preclusive of sheer panic fright.

But Beckford remained alone in his devotion to the Orient. Other writers, closer to the Gothic tradition and to European life in general, were content to follow more faithfully in the lead of Walpole. Among the countless producers of terror-literature in these times may be mentioned the Utopian economic theorist William Godwin, who followed his famous but non-supernatural *Caleb Williams* (1794) with the intendedly weird *St. Leon* (1799), in which the theme of the elixir of life, as developed by the imaginary secret order of "Rosicrucians," is handled with ingeniousness if not with atmospheric convincingness. This element of Rosicrucianism, fostered by a wave of popular magical interest exemplified in the vogue of the charlatan Cagliostro and the publication of Francis Barrett's *The Magus* (1801), a curious and compendious treatise on occult principles and ceremonies, of which a reprint was made as lately as 1896, figures in Bulwer-Lytton and in many late Gothic novels, especially that remote and enfeebled posterity which straggled far down into the nineteenth century and was represented by George W.M. Reynold's *Faust and the Demon* and *Wagner the Wehr-Wolf*. *Caleb Williams*, though non-supernatural, has many authentic touches of terror. It is the tale of a servant persecuted by a master whom he has found guilty of murder, and displays an invention and skill which have kept it alive in a fashion to this day. It was dramatized as *The Iron Chest*, and in that form was almost equally celebrated. Godwin, however, was too much the conscious teacher and prosaic man of thought to create a genuine weird masterpiece.

His daughter, the wife of Shelley, was much more successful; and her inimitable *Frankenstein; or, the Modern Prometheus* (1817) is one of the horror-classics of all time. Composed in competition with her husband, Lord Byron, and Dr. John William Polidori in an effort to prove supremacy in horror-making, Mrs. Shelley's *Frankenstein* was the only one of the rival narratives to be brought to an elaborate completion; and criticism has failed to prove that the best parts are due to Shelley rather than to her. The novel, somewhat tinged but scarcely marred by moral didacticism, tells of the artificial human being moulded from charnel fragments by Victor Frankenstein, a young Swiss medical student. Created by its designer "in the mad pride of intellectuality," the monster possesses full intelligence but owns a hideously loathsome form. It is rejected by mankind, becomes embittered, and at length begins the successive murder of all whom Frankenstein loves best, friends and family. It demands that Frankenstein create a wife for it; and when the student finally refuses in horror lest the world be populated with such monsters, it departs with a hideous threat "to be with him on his wedding night." Upon that night the bride is strangled, and from that time on Frankenstein hunts down the monster, even into the wastes of the Arctic. In the end, whilst seeking shelter on the ship of the man who tells the story, Frankenstein himself is killed by the shocking object of his search and creation of his presumptuous pride. Some of the scenes in *Frankenstein* are unforgettable, as when the newly animated monster enters its creator's room, parts the curtains of his bed, and gazes at him in the yellow moonlight with watery eyes — "if eyes they may be called." Mrs. Shelley wrote other novels, including the fairly notable *Last Man;* but never duplicated the success of her first effort. It has the true touch of cosmic fear, no matter how much the movement may lag in places. Dr. Polidori developed his competing idea as a long short story, *The Vampyre;* in which we behold a suave villain of the true Gothic or Byronic type, and encounter some excellent passages of stark fright, including a terrible nocturnal experience in a shunned Grecian wood.

In this same period Sir Walter Scott frequently concerned himself with the weird, weaving it into many of his novels and poems, and sometimes producing such independent bits of narration as *The Tapestried Chamber* or *Wandering Willie's Tale* in *Redgauntlet,* in the latter of which the force of the spectral and the diabolic is enhanced by a grotesque homeliness of speech and atmosphere. In 1830 Scott published his *Letters on Demonology and Witchcraft,* which still forms one of our best compendia of European witchlore. Washington Irving is another famous figure not unconnected with the weird; for though most of his ghosts are too whimsical and humorous to form genuinely spectral literature, a distinct inclination in this direction is to be noted in many of his productions. *The German Student* in *Tales of a Traveler* (1824) is a slyly concise and effective presentation of the old legend of the dead bride, whilst woven into the cosmic tissue of *The Money Diggers* in the same volume is more than one hint of piratical apparitions in the realms which Captain Kidd once roamed. Thomas Moore also joined the ranks of the macabre artists in the poem *Alciphron,* which he later elaborated into the prose novel of

The Epicurean (1827). Though merely relating the adventures of a young Athenian duped by the artifice of cunning Egyptian priests, Moore manages to infuse much genuine horror into his account of subterranean frights and wonders beneath the primordial temples of Memphis. De Quincey more than once revels in grotesque and arabesque terrors, though with a desultoriness and learned pomp which deny him the rank of specialist.

This era likewise saw the rise of William Harrison Ainsworth, whose romantic novels teem with the eerie and the gruesome. Capt. Marryat, besides writing such short tales as *The Werewolf*, made a memorable contribution in *The Phantom Ship* (1839), founded on the legend of the Flying Dutchman, whose spectral and accursed vessel sails for ever near the Cape of Good Hope. Dickens now rises with occasional weird bits like *The Signalman*, a tale of ghastly warning conforming to a very common pattern and touched with a verisimilitude which allied it as much with the coming psychological school as with the dying Gothic school. At this time a wave of interest in spiritualistic charlatanry, mediumism, Hindoo theosophy, and such matters, much like that of the present day, was flourishing; so that the number of weird tales with a "Psychic" or pseudo-scientific basis became very considerable. For a number of these the prolific and popular Edward Bulwer-Lytton was responsible; and despite the large doses of turgid rhetoric and empty romanticism in his products, his success in the weaving of a certain kind of bizarre charm cannot be denied.

The House and the Brain, which hints of Rosicrucianism and at a malign and deathless figure perhaps suggested by Louis XV's mysterious courtier St. Germain, yet survives as one of the best short haunted-house tales ever written. The novel *Zanoni* (1842) contains similar elements more elaborately handled, and introduces a vast unknown sphere of being pressing on our own world and guarded by a horrible "Dweller of the Threshold" who haunts those who try to enter and fail. Here we have a benign brotherhood kept alive from age to age till finally reduced to a single member, and as a hero an ancient Chaldaean sorcerer surviving in the pristine bloom of youth to perish on the guillotine of the French Revolution. Though full of the conventional spirit of romance, marred by a ponderous network of symbolic and didactic meanings, and left unconvincing through lack of perfect atmospheric realization of the situations hinging on the spectral world, *Zanoni* is really an excellent performance as a romantic novel; and can be read with genuine interest by the not too sophisticated reader. It is amusing to note that in describing an attempted initiation into the ancient brotherhood the author cannot escape using the stock Gothic castle of Walpolian lineage.

In *A Strange Story* (1862) Bulwer-Lytton shows a marked improvement in the creation of weird images and moods. The novel, despite enormous length, a highly artificial plot bolstered up by opportune coincidences, and an atmosphere of homiletic pseudo-science designed to please the matter-of-fact and purposeful Victorian reader, is exceedingly effective as a narrative; evoking instantaneous and unflagging interest, and furnishing many potent — if somewhat melodramatic — tableaux and climaxes. Again we have the mysterious user of life's elixir in the person of the soulless magician Margrave, whose dark exploits stand out with dramatic vividness against the modern background of a quiet English town and of the Australian bush; and again we have shadowy intimations of a vast spectral world of the unknown in the very air about us — this time handled with much greater power and vitality than in *Zanoni*. One of the two great incantation passages, where the hero is driven by a luminous evil spirit to rise at night in his sleep, take a strange Egyptian wand, and evoke nameless presences in the haunted and mausoleum-facing pavilion of a famous Renaissance alchemist, truly stands among the major terror scenes of literature. Just enough is suggested, and just little enough is told. Unknown words are twice dictated to the sleep-walker, and as he repeats them the ground trembles, and all the dogs of the country-side begin to bay at half-seen amorphous shadows that stalk athwart the moonlight. When a third set of unknown words is prompted, the sleep-walker's spirit suddenly rebels at uttering them, as if the soul could recognize ultimate abysmal horrors concealed from the mind; and at last an apparition of an absent sweetheart and good angel breaks the malign spell. This fragment well illustrates how far Lord Lytton was capable of progressing beyond his usual pomp and stock romance toward that crystalline essence of artistic fear which belongs to the domain of poetry. In describing certain details of incantations, Lytton was greatly indebted to his amusingly serious occult studies, in the course of which he came in touch with that odd French scholar and cabalist Alphonse Louis Constant ("Eliphas Levy"), who claimed to possess the secrets of ancient magic, and to have evoked the spectre of the old Grecian wizard Apollonius of Tyana, who lived in Nero's times.

The romantic, semi-Gothic, quasi-moral tradition here

represented was carried far down the nineteenth century by such authors as Joseph Sheridan LeFanu, Wilkie Collins, the late Sir H. Rider Haggard (whose *She* is really remarkably good), Sir A. Conan Doyle, H. G. Wells, and Robert Louis Stevenson — the latter of whom, despite an atrocious tendency toward jaunty mannerisms, created permanent classics in *Markheim,The Body Snatcher,* and *Dr. Jekyll and Mr. Hyde.* Indeed, we may say that this school still survives; for to it clearly belong such of our contemporary horror-tales as specialise in events rather than atmospheric details, address the intellect rather than a malign tensity or psychological verisimilitude, and take a definite stand in sympathy with mankind and its welfare. It has its undeniable strength, and because of its "human element" commands a wider audience than does the sheer artistic nightmare. If not quite so potent as the latter, it is because a diluted product can never achieve the intensity of a concentrated essence.

Quite alone both as a novel and as a piece of terror-literature stands the famous *Wuthering Heights* (1847) by Emily Brontë, with its mad vistas of bleak, windswept Yorkshire moors and the violent, distorted lives they foster. Though primarily a tale of life, and of human passions in agony and conflict, its epically cosmic setting affords room for horror of the most spiritual sort. Heathcliff, the modified Byronic villain-hero, is a strange dark waif found in the streets as a small child and speaking only a strange gibberish till adopted by the family he ultimately ruins. That he is in truth a diabolic spirit rather than a human being is more than once suggested, and the unreal is further approached in the experience of the visitor who encounters a plaintive child-ghost at a bough-brushed upper window. Between Heathcliff and

Catherine Earnshaw is a tie deeper and more terrible than human love. After her death he twice disturbs her grave, and is haunted by an impalpable presence which can be nothing less than her spirit. The spirit enters his life more and more, and at last he becomes confident of some imminent mystical reunion. He says he feels a strange change approaching, and ceases to take nourishment. At night he either walks abroad or opens the casement by his bed. When he dies the casement is still swinging open to the pouring rain, and a queer smile pervades the stiffened face. They bury him in a grave beside the mound he has haunted for eighteen years, and small shepherd boys say that he yet walks with his Catherine in the churchyard and on the moor when it rains. Their faces, too, are sometimes seen on rainy nights behind that upper casement at Wuthering Heights. Miss Brontë's eerie terror is no mere Gothic echo, but a tense expression of man's shuddering reaction to the unknown. In this respect, *Wuthering Heights* becomes the symbol of a literary transition, and marks the growth of a new and sounder school.

VI.

Spectral Literature On The Continent

ON the continent literary horror fared well. The celebrated short tales and novels of Ernst Theodor Amadeus Hoffmann (1776-1822) are a by-word for mellowness of background and maturity of form, though they incline to levity and extravagance, and lack the exalted moments of stark, breathless terror which a less sophisticated writer might have achieved. Generally they convey the grotesque rather than the terrible. Most artistic of all the continental weird tales is the German classic *Undine* (1814), by Friedrich Heinrich Karl, Baron de la Motte Fouqué;. In this story of a water-spirit who married a mortal and gained a human soul there is a delicate fineness of craftsmanship which makes it notable in any department of literature, and an easy naturalness which places it close to the genuine folk-myth. It is, in fact, derived from a tale told by the Renaissance physician and alchemist Paracelsus in his *Treatise on Elemental Sprites.*

Undine, daughter of a powerful water-prince, was exchanged by her father as a small child for a fisherman's daughter, in order that she might acquire a soul by wedding a human being. Meeting the noble youth Huldbrand at the cottage of her fosterfather by the sea at the edge of a haunted wood, she soon marries him, and accompanies him to his ancestral castle of Ringstetten. Huldbrand, however, eventually wearies of his wife's supernatural affiliations, and especially of the appearances of her uncle, the malicious woodland waterfall-spirit Kuhleborn; a weariness increased by his growing affection for Bertalda, who turns out to be the fisherman's child for whom Undine was changed. At length, on a voyage down the Danube, he is provoked by some innocent act of his devoted wife to utter the angry words which consign her back to her supernatural element; from which she can, by the laws of her species, return only once — to kill him, whether she will or no, if ever he prove unfaithful to her memory. Later, when Huldbrand is about to be married to Bertalda, Undine returns for her sad duty, and bears his life away in tears. When he is buried among his fathers in the village churchyard a veiled, snow-white female figure appears among the mourners, but after the prayer is seen no more. In her place is seen a little silver spring, which murmurs its way almost completely around the new grave, and empties into a neighboring lake. The villagers show it to this day, and say that Undine and her Huldbrand are thus united in death. Many passages and atmospheric touches in this tale reveal Fouqué as an accomplished artist in the field of the macabre; especially the descriptions of the haunted wood with its gigantic snow-white man and various unnamed terrors, which occur early in the narrative.

Not so well known as *Undine*, but remarkable for its convincing realism and freedom from Gothic stock devices, is the *Amber Witch* of Wilhelm Meinhold, another product of the German fantastic genius of the earlier nineteenth century. This tale, which is laid in the time of the Thirty Years' War, purports to be a clergyman's manuscript found in an old church at Coserow, and centres round the writer's daughter, Maria Schweidler, who is wrongly accused of witchcraft. She has found a deposit of amber which she keeps secret for various reasons, and the unexplained wealth obtained from this lends colour to the accusation; an accusation instigated by the malice of the wolf-hunting nobleman Wittich Appelmann, who has vainly pursued her with ignoble designs. The deeds of a real witch, who afterward comes to a horrible supernatural end in prison, are glibly imputed to the hapless Maria; and after a typical witchcraft trial with forced confessions under torture she is about to be burned at the stake when saved just in time by her lover, a noble youth from a neighboring district. Meinhold's great strength is in his air of casual and realistic verisimilitude, which intensifies our suspense and sense of the unseen by half persuading us that the menacing events must somehow be either the truth or very dose to the truth. Indeed, so thorough is this realism that a popular magazine once published the main points of *The Amber Witch* as an actual occurrence of the seventeenth century!

In the present generation German horror-fiction is most notably represented by Hanns Heinz Ewers, who brings to bear on his dark conceptions an effective knowledge of modern psychology. Novels like *The Sorcerer's Apprentice* and *Alrune,* and short stories like *The Spider,* contain distinctive qualities which raise them to a classic level.

But France as well as Germany has been active in the realm of weirdness. Victor Hugo, in such tales as *Hans of Iceland,* and Balzac, in *The Wild Ass's Skin, Seraphita,* and *Louis Lambert,* both employ supernaturalism to a greater or less extent; though generally only as a means to some more human end, and without the sincere and dæmonic intensity which characterizes the born artist in shadows. It is in Theophile Gautier that we first seem to find an authentic French sense of the unreal world, and here there appears a spectral mystery which, though not continuously used, is recognizable at once as something alike genuine and profound. Short tales like *Avatar, The Foot of the Mummy,* and *Clarimonde* display glimpses of forbidden vistas that allure, tantalize, and sometime horrify; whilst the Egyptian visions evoked in *One of Cleopatra's Nights* are of the keenest and most expressive potency. Gautier captured the inmost soul of æon-weighted Egypt, with its cryptic life and Cyclopean architecture, and uttered once and for all the eternal horror of its nether world of catacombs, where to the end of time millions of stiff, spiced corpses will stare up in the blackness with glassy eyes, awaiting some awesome and unrelatable summons. Gustave Flaubert ably continued the tradition of Gautier in orgies of poetic phantasy like *The Temptation of St. Anthony,* and but for a strong realistic bias might have been an arch-weaver of tapestried terrors. Later on we see the stream divide, producing strange poets and fantaisistes of the symbolic and decadent schools whose dark interests really centre more in abnormalities of human thought and instinct than in the actual supernatural, and subtle story-tellers whose thrills are quite directly derived from the night-black wells of cosmic unreality. Of the former class of "artists in sin" the illustrious poet Baudelaire, influenced vastly by Poe, is the supreme type; whilst the psychological novelist Joris-Karl Huysmans, a true child of the eighteen-nineties, is at once the summation and finale. The latter and purely narrative class is continued by Prosper Merimée, whose *Venus of Ille* presents in terse and convincing prose the same ancient statue-bride theme which Thomas Moore cast in ballad form in *The Ring.*

The horror-tales of the powerful and cynical Guy de Maupassant, written as his final madness gradually over-took him, present individualities of their own; being rather the morbid outpourings of a realistic mind in a pathological state than the healthy imaginative products of a vision natu-rally disposed toward phantasy and sensitive to the normal illusions of the unseen. Nevertheless they are of the keenest interest and poignancy; suggesting with marvelous force the imminence of nameless terrors, and the relentless dog-ging of an ill-starred individual by hideous and menacing representatives of the outer blackness. Of these stories *The*

Horla is generally regarded as the masterpiece. Relating the advent to France of an invisible being who lives on water and milk, sways the minds of others, and seems to be the vanguard of a horde of extra-terrestrial organisms arrived on earth to subjugate and overwhelm mankind, this tense narrative is perhaps without a peer in its particular department; notwithstanding its indebtedness to a tale by the American Fitz-James O'Brien for details in describing the actual presence of the unseen monster. Other potently dark creations of de Maupassant are *Who Knows?*, *The Spectre*, *He*, *The Diary of a Madman*, *The White Wolf*, *On the River*, and the grisly verses entitled *Horror*.

The collaborators Erckmann-Chatrian enriched French literature with many spectral fancies like *The Man-Wolf*, in which a transmitted curse works toward its end in a traditional Gothic-castle setting. Their power of creating a shuddering midnight atmosphere was tremendous despite a tendency toward natural explanations and scientific wonders; and few short tales contain greater horror than *The Invisible Eye*, where a malignant old hag weaves nocturnal hypnotic spells which induce the successive occupants of a certain inn chamber to hang themselves on a cross-beam. *The Owl's Ear* and *The Waters of Death* are full of engulfing darkness and mystery, the latter embodying the familiar over-grown-spider theme so frequently employed by weird fictionists. Villiers de l'Isle Adam likewise followed the macabre school; his *Torture by Hope*, the tale of a stake-condemned prisoner permitted to escape in order to feel the pangs of recapture, being held by some to constitute the most harrowing short story in literature. This type, however, is less a part of the weird tradition than a class peculiar to itself — the so-called *conte cruel*, in which the wrenching of the emotions is accomplished through dramatic tantalizations, frustrations, and gruesome physical horrors. Almost wholly devoted to this form is the living writer Maurice Level, whose very brief episodes have lent themselves so readily to theatrical adaptation in the "thrillers" of the Grand Guignol. As a matter of fact, the French genius is more naturally suited to this dark realism than to the suggestion of the unseen; since the latter process requires, for its best and most sympathetic development on a large scale, the inherent mysticism of the Northern mind.

A very flourishing, though till recently quite hidden, branch of weird literature is that of the Jews, kept alive and nourished in obscurity by the sombre heritage of early Eastern magic, apocalyptic literature, and cabbalism. The Semitic mind, like the Celtic and Teutonic, seems to possess marked mystical inclinations; and the wealth of underground horror-lore surviving in ghettoes and synagogues must be much more considerable than is generally imagined. Cabbalism itself, so prominent during the Middle Ages, is a system of philosophy explaining the universe as emanations of the Deity, and involving the existence of strange spiritual realms and beings apart from the visible world of which dark glimpses may be obtained through certain secret incantations. Its ritual is bound up with mystical interpretations of the Old Testament, and attributes an esoteric significance to each letter of the Hebrew alphabet — a circumstance which has imparted to Hebrew letters a sort of spectral glamour and potency in the popular literature of magic. Jewish folklore has preserved much of the terror and mystery of the past, and when more thoroughly studied is likely to exert considerable influence on weird fiction. The best examples of its literary use so far are the German novel *The Golem*, by Gustave Meyrink, and the drama *The Dybbuk*, by the Jewish writer using the pseudonym "Ansky." The former, with its haunting shadowy suggestions of marvels and horrors just beyond reach, is laid in Prague, and describes with singular mastery that city's ancient ghetto with its spectral, peaked gables. The name is derived from a fabulous artificial giant supposed to be made and animated by mediæval rabbis according to a certain cryptic formula. *The Dybbuk*, translated and produced in America in 1925, and more recently produced as an opera, describes with singular power the possession of a living body by the evil soul of a dead man. Both golems and dybbuks are fixed types, and serve as frequent ingredients of later Jewish tradition.

VII.
Edgar Allan Poe

IN the eighteen-thirties occurred a literary dawn directly affecting not only the history of the weird tale, but that of short fiction as a whole; and indirectly moulding the trends and fortunes of a great European æsthetic school. It is our good fortune as Americans to be able to claim that dawn as our own, for it came in the person of our most illustrious and unfortunate fellow-countryman Edgar Allan Poe. Poe's fame has been subject to curious undulations, and it is now a fashion amongst the "advanced intelligentsia" to minimize his importance both as an artist and as an influence; but it would be hard for any mature and reflective critic to deny the tremendous value of his work and the persuasive potency of his mind as an opener of artistic vistas. True, his type of outlook may have been anticipated; but it was he who first realized its possibilities and gave it supreme form and systematic expression. True also, that subsequent writers may have produced greater single tales than his; but again we must comprehend that it was only he who taught them by example and precept the art which they, having the way cleared for them and given an explicit guide, were perhaps able to carry to greater lengths. Whatever his limitations, Poe did that which no one else ever did or could have done; and to him we owe the modern horror-story in its final and perfected state.

Before Poe the bulk of weird writers had worked largely in the dark; without an understanding of the psychological basis of the horror appeal, and hampered by more or less the need for conformity to certain empty literary conventions such as the happy ending, virtue rewarded, and in general a hollow moral didacticism, acceptance of popular standards and values, and striving of the author to obtrude his own emotions into the story and take sides with the partisans of the majority's artificial ideas. Poe, on the other hand, perceived the essential impersonality of the real artist; and knew that the function of creative fiction is merely to express and interpret events and sensations as they are, regardless of how they tend or what they prove — good or evil, attractive or repulsive, stimulating or depressing, with the author always acting as a vivid and detached chronicler rather than as a teacher, sympathizer, or vendor of opinion. He saw clearly that all phases of life and thought are equally eligible as a subject matter for the artist, and being inclined by temperament to strangeness and gloom, decided to be the interpreter of those powerful feelings and frequent happenings which attend pain rather than pleasure, decay rather than growth, terror rather than tranquility, and which are fundamentally either adverse or indifferent to the tastes and traditional outward sentiments of mankind, and to the health, sanity, and normal expansive welfare of the species.

Poe's spectres thus acquired a convincing malignity possessed by none of their predecessors, and established a new standard of realism in the annals of literary horror. The impersonal and artistic intent, moreover, was aided by a scientific attitude not often found before; whereby Poe studied the human mind rather than the usages of Gothic fiction, and worked with an analytical knowledge of terror's true sources which doubled the force of his narratives and emancipated him from all the absurdities inherent in merely conventional shudder-coining. This example having been set, later authors were naturally forced to conform to it in order to compete at all; so that in this way a definite change began to affect the main stream of macabre writing. Poe, too, set a fashion in consummate craftsmanship; and although today some of his own work seems slightly melodramatic and unsophisticated, we can constantly trace his influence in such things as the maintenance of a single mood and achievement of a single impression in a tale, and the rigorous paring down of incidents to such as have a direct bearing on the plot and will figure prominently in the climax. Truly may it be said that Poe invented the short story in its present form. His elevation of disease, perversity, and decay to the level of artistically expressible themes was likewise infinitely far-reaching in effect; for avidly seized, sponsored, and intensified by his eminent French admirer Charles Pierre Baudelaire, it became the nucleus of the principal æsthetic movements in France, thus making Poe in a sense the father of the Decadents and the Symbolists.

Poet and critic by nature and supreme attainment, logician and philosopher by taste and mannerism, Poe was by no means immune from defects and affectations. His pretence to profound and obscure scholarship, his blundering ventures in stilted and laboured pseudo-humor, and his often vitriolic outbursts of critical prejudice must all be recognized and forgiven. Beyond and above them, and dwarfing them to insignificance, was a master's vision of the terror that stalks about and within us, and the worm that writhes and slavers in the hideously close abyss. Penetrating to every festering horror in the gaily painted mockery called existence, and in the solemn masquerade called human thought and feeling, that vision had power to project itself in blackly magical crystallisations and transmutations; till there bloomed in the sterile America of the thirties and forties such a moon-nourished garden of gorgeous poison fungi as not even the nether slopes of Saturn might boast. Verses and tales alike sustain the burthen of cosmic panic. The raven whose noisome beak pierces the heart, the ghouls that toll iron bells in pestilential steeples, the vault of Ulalume in the black October night, the shocking spires and domes under the sea, the "wild, weird clime that lieth, sublime, out of Space — out of Time" — all these things and more leer at us amidst maniacal rattlings in the seething nightmare of the poetry. And in the prose there yawn open for us the very jaws of the pit — inconceivable abnormalities slyly hinted into a horrible half-knowledge by words whose innocence we scarcely doubt till the cracked tension of the speaker's hollow voice bids us fear their nameless implications; dæmoniac patterns and presences slumbering noxiously till waked for one phobic instant into a shrieking revelation that cackles itself to sudden madness or explodes in memorable and cataclysmic echoes. A Witches' Sabbath of horror flinging off decorous robes is flashed before us — a sight the more monstrous because of the scientific skill with which every particular is marshaled and brought into an easy apparent relation to the known gruesomeness of material life.

Poe's tales, of course, fall into several classes; some of which contain a purer essence of spiritual horror than others. The tales of logic and ratiocination, forerunners of the modern detective story, are not to be included at all in weird literature; whilst certain others, probably influenced considerably by Hoffmann, possess an extravagance which relegates them to the borderline of the grotesque. Still a third group deal with abnormal psychology and monomania in such a way as to express terror but not weirdness. A substantial residuum, however, represent the literature of supernatural horror in its acutest form; and give their author a permanent and unassailable place as deity and fountainhead of all modern diabolic fiction. Who can forget the terrible swollen ship poised on the billow-chasm's edge in *MS. Found in a Bottle* — the dark intimations of her unhallowed age and monstrous growth, her sinister crew of unseeing greybeards, and her frightful southward rush under full sail through the ice of the Antarctic night, sucked onward by some resistless devil-current toward a vortex of eldritch enlightenment which must end in destruction?

Then there is the unutterable *M. Valdemar,* kept together
by hypnotism for seven months after his death, and uttering
frantic sounds but a moment before the breaking of the spell
leaves him "a nearly liquid mass of loathsome, of detestable
putrescence." In the *Narrative of A. Gordon Pym* the voyagers
reach first a strange south polar land of murderous savages
where nothing is white and where vast rocky ravines have
the form of titanic Egyptian letters spelling terrible primal
arcana of earth; and thereafter a still more mysterious realm
where everything is white, and where shrouded giants and
snowy-plumed birds guard a cryptic cataract of mist which
empties from immeasurable celestial heights into a torrid
milky sea. *Metzengerstein* horrifies with its malign hints of
a monstrous metempsychosis — the mad nobleman who
burns the stable of his hereditary foe; the colossal unknown
horse that issues from the blazing building after the owner
has perished therein; the vanishing bit of ancient tapestry
where was shown the giant horse of the victim's ancestor in
the Crusades; the madman's wild and constant riding on the
great horse, and his fear and hatred of the steed; the meaningless prophecies that brood obscurely over the warring
houses; and finally, the burning of the madman's palace and
the death therein of the owner, borne helpless into the
flames and up the vast staircase astride the beast he had
ridden so strangely. Afterward the rising smoke of the ruins
takes the form of a gigantic horse. *The Man of the Crowd,*
telling of one who roams day and night to mingle with
streams of people as if afraid to be alone, has quieter effects,
but implies nothing less of cosmic fear. Poe's mind was
never far from terror and decay, and we see in every tale,
poem, and philosophical dialogue a tense eagerness to

fathom unplumbed wells of night, to pierce the veil of death, and to reign in fancy as lord of the frightful mysteries of time and space.

Certain of Poe's tales possess an almost absolute perfection of artistic form which makes them veritable beacon-lights in the province of the short story. Poe could, when he wished, give to his prose a richly poetic cast; employing that archaic and Orientalised style with jeweled phrase, quasi-Biblical repetition, and recurrent burthen so successfully used by later writers like Oscar Wilde and Lord Dunsany; and in the cases where he has done this we have an effect of lyrical phantasy almost narcotic in essence — an opium pageant of dream in the language of dream, with every unnatural colour and grotesque image bodied forth in a symphony of corresponding sound. The *Masque of the Red Death, Silence, a Fable,* and *Shadow, a Parable,* are assuredly poems in every sense of the word save the metrical one, and owe as much of their power to aural cadence as to visual imagery. But it is in two of the less openly poetic tales, *Ligeia* and *The Fall of the House of Usher* — especially the latter — that one finds those very summits of artistry whereby Poe takes his place at the head of fictional miniaturists. Simple and straightforward in plot, both of these tales owe their supreme magic to the cunning development which appears in the selection and collocation of every least incident. *Ligeia* tells of a first wife of lofty and mysterious origin, who after death returns through a preternatural force of will to take possession of the body of a second wife; imposing even her physical appearance on the temporary reanimated corpse of her victim at the last moment. Despite a suspicion of pro-lixity and topheaviness, the narrative reaches its terrific climax with relentless power. *Usher,* whose superiority in detail and proportion is very marked, hints shudderingly of obscure life in inorganic things, and displays an abnormally linked trinity of entities at the end of a long and isolated family history — a brother, his twin sister, and their incredibly ancient house all sharing a single soul and meeting one common dissolution at the same moment.

These bizarre conceptions, so awkward in unskillful hands, become under Poe's spell living and convincing terrors to haunt our nights; and all because the author understood so perfectly the very mechanics and physiology of fear and strangeness — the essential details to emphasise, the precise incongruities and conceits to select as preliminaries or concomitants to horror, the exact incidents and allusions to throw out innocently in advance as symbols or prefigurings of each major step toward the hideous *dénouement* to come, the nice adjustments of cumulative force and the unerring accuracy in linkage of parts which make for faultless unity throughout and thunderous effectiveness at the climactic moment, the delicate nuances of scenic and landscape value to select in establishing and sustaining the desired mood and vitalising the desired illusion — principles of this kind, and dozens of obscurer ones too elusive to be described or even fully comprehended by any ordinary commentator. Melodrama and unsophistication there may be — we are told of one fastidious Frenchman who could not bear to read Poe except in Baudelaire's urbane and Gallically modulated translation — but all traces of such things are wholly overshadowed by a potent and inborn sense of the spectral, the morbid, and the horrible which gushed forth from every cell of the artist's creative mentality and stamped his macabre work with the ineffaceable mark of supreme genius. Poe's weird tales are *alive* in a manner that few others can ever hope to be.

Like most fantaisistes, Poe excels in incidents and broad narrative effects rather than in character drawing. His typical protagonist is generally a dark, handsome, proud, melancholy, intellectual, highly sensitive, capricious, introspective, isolated, and sometimes slightly mad gentleman of ancient family and opulent circumstances; usually deeply learned in strange lore, and darkly ambitious of penetrating to forbidden secrets of the universe. Aside from a high-sounding name, this character obviously derives little from the early Gothic novel; for he is clearly neither the wooden hero nor the diabolical villain of Radcliffian or Ludovician romance. Indirectly, however, he does possess a sort of genealogical connection; since his gloomy, ambitious and anti-social qualities savour strongly of the typical Byronic hero, who in turn is definitely an offspring of the Gothic Manfreds, Montonis, and Ambrosios. More particular qualities appear to be derived from the psychology of Poe himself, who certainly possessed much of the depression, sensitiveness, mad aspiration, loneliness, and extravagant freakishness which he attributes to his haughty and solitary victims of Fate.

VIII.
The Weird Tradition in America

THE public for whom Poe wrote, though grossly unappreciative of his art, was by no means unaccustomed to the horrors with which he dealt. America, besides inheriting the usual dark folklore of Europe, had an additional fund of weird associations to draw upon; so that spectral legends had already been recognised as fruitful subject-matter for literature. Charles Brockden Brown had achieved phenomenal fame with his Radcliffian romances, and Washington Irving's lighter treatment of eerie themes had quickly become classic. This additional fund proceeded, as Paul Elmer More has pointed out, from the keen spiritual and theological interests of the first colonists, plus the strange and forbidding nature of the scene into which they were plunged. The vast and gloomy virgin forests in whose perpetual twilight all terrors might well lurk; the hordes of coppery Indians whose strange, saturnine visages and violent customs hinted strongly at traces of infernal origin; the free rein given under the influence of Puritan theocracy to all manner of notions respecting man's relation to the stern and vengeful God of the Calvinists, and to the sulphureous Adversary of that God, about whom so much was thundered in the pulpits each Sunday; and the morbid introspection developed by an isolated backwoods life devoid of normal amusements and of the recreational mood, harassed by commands for theological self-examination, keyed to unnatural emotional repression, and forming above all a mere grim struggle for survival — all these things conspired to produce an environment in which the black whisperings of sinister grandams were heard far beyond the chimney corner, and in which tales of witchcraft and unbelievable secret monstrosities lingered long after the dread days of the Salem nightmare.

Poe represents the newer, more disillusioned, and more technically finished of the weird schools that rose out of this propitious milieu. Another school — the tradition of moral values, gentle restraint, and mild, leisurely phantasy tinged more or less with the whimsical — was represented by another famous, misunderstood, and lonely figure in American letters — the shy and sensitive Nathaniel Hawthorne, scion of antique Salem and great-grandson of one of the bloodiest of the old witchcraft judges. In Hawthorne we have none of the violence, the daring, the high colouring, the intense dramatic sense, the cosmic malignity, and the undivided and impersonal artistry of Poe. Here, instead, is a gentle soul cramped by the Puritanism of early New England; shadowed and wistful, and grieved at an unmoral universe which everywhere transcends the conventional patterns thought by our forefathers to represent divine and immutable law. Evil, a very real force to Hawthorne, appears on every hand as a lurking and conquering adversary; and the visible world becomes in his fancy a theatre of infinite tragedy and woe, with unseen half-existent influences hovering over it and through it, battling for supremacy and moulding the destinies of the hapless mortals who form its vain and self-deluded population. The heritage of American weirdness was his to a most intense degree, and he saw a dismal throng of vague specters behind the common phenomena of life; but he was not disinterested enough to value impressions, sensations, and beauties of narration for their own sake. He must needs weave his phantasy into some quietly melancholy fabric of didactic or allegorical cast, in which his meekly resigned cynicism may display with naïve moral appraisal the perfidy of a human race which he cannot cease to cherish and mourn despite his insight into its hypocrisy. Supernatural horror, then, is never a primary object with Hawthorne; though its impulses were so deeply woven into his personality that he cannot help suggesting it with the force of genius when he calls upon the unreal world to illustrate the pensive sermon he wishes to preach.

Hawthorne's intimations of the weird, always gentle, elusive, and restrained, may be traced throughout his work. The mood that produced them found one delightful vent in the Teutonised retelling of classic myths for children contained in *A Wonder Book* and *Tanglewood Tales,* and at other times exercised itself in casting a certain strangeness and intangible witchery or malevolence over events not meant to be actually supernatural; as in the macabre posthumous novel *Dr. Grimshawe's Secret,* which invests with a peculiar sort of repulsion a house existing to this day in Salem, and abutting on the ancient Charter Street Burying Ground. In *The Marble Faun,* whose design was sketched out in an Italian villa reputed to be haunted, a tremendous background of genuine phantasy and mystery palpitates just beyond the common reader's sight; and glimpses of fabulous blood in mortal veins are hinted at during the course of a romance which cannot help being interesting despite the persistent incubus of moral allegory, anti-Popery propaganda, and a Puritan prudery which has caused the modern writer D. H. Lawrence to express a longing to treat the author in a highly undignified manner. *Septimius Felton,* a posthumous novel whose idea was to have been elaborated and incorporated into the unfinished *Dolliver Romance,* touches on the Elixir of Life in a more or less capable fashion whilst the notes for a never-written tale to be called *The Ancestral Footstep* show what Hawthorne would have done with an intensive treatment of an old English superstition —

that of an ancient and accursed line whose members left footprints of blood as they walked — which appears incidentally in both *Septimius Felton* and *Dr. Grimshawe's Secret*.

Many of Hawthorne's shorter tales exhibit weirdness, either of atmosphere or of incident, to a remarkable degree. *Edward Randolph's Portrait*, in *Legends of the Province House*, has its diabolic moments. *The Minister's Black Veil* (founded on an actual incident) and *The Ambitious Guest* imply much more than they state, whilst *Ethan Grand* — a fragment of a longer work never completed — rises to genuine heights of cosmic fear with its vignette of the wild hill country and the blazing, desolate lime-kilns, and its delineation of the Byronic "unpardonable sinner," whose troubled life ends with a peal of fearful laughter in the night as he seeks rest amidst the flames of the furnace. Some of Hawthorne's notes tell of weird tales he would have written had he lived longer — an especially vivid plot being that concerning a baffling stranger who appeared now and then in public assemblies, and who was at last followed and found to come and go from a very ancient grave.

But foremost as a finished, artistic unit among all our author's weird material is the famous and exquisitely wrought novel, *The House of the Seven Gables*, in which the relentless working out of an ancestral curse is developed with astonishing power against the sinister background of a very ancient Salem house — one of those peaked Gothic affairs which formed the first regular building-up of our New England coast towns but which gave way after the seventeenth century to the more familiar gambrel-roofed or classic Georgian types now known as "Colonial." Of these old gabled Gothic houses scarcely a dozen are to be seen today in their original condition throughout the United States, but one well known to Hawthorne still stands in Turner Street, Salem, and is pointed out with doubtful authority as the scene and inspiration of the romance. Such an edifice, with its spectral peaks, its clustered chimneys, its overhanging second story, its grotesque corner-brackets, and its diamond-paned lattice windows, is indeed an object well calculated to evoke sombre reflections; typifying as it does the dark Puritan age of concealed horror and witch-whispers which preceded the beauty, rationality, and spaciousness of the eighteenth century. Hawthorne saw many in his youth, and knew the black tales connected with some of them. He heard, too, many rumours of a curse upon his own line as the result of his great-grandfather's severity as a witchcraft judge in 1692.

From this setting came the immortal tale — New England's greatest contribution to weird literature — and we can feel in an instant the authenticity of the atmosphere presented to us. Stealthy horror and disease lurk within the weather-blackened, moss-crusted, and elm-shadowed walls of the archaic dwelling so vividly displayed, and we grasp the brooding malignity of the place when we read that its builder — old Colonel Pyncheon — snatched the land with peculiar ruthlessness from its original settler, Matthew Maule, whom he condemned to the gallows as a wizard in the year of the panic. Maule died cursing old Pyncheon — "God will give him blood to drink" — and the waters of the old well on the seized land turned bitter. Maule's carpenter son consented to build the great gabled house for his fathet's triumphant enemy, but the old Colonel died strangely on the day of its dedication. Then followed generations of odd vicissitudes, with queer whispers about the dark powers of the Maules, and sometimes terrible ends befalling the Pyncheons.

The overshadowing malevolence of the ancient house — almost as alive as Poe's House of Usher, though in a subtler way — pervades the tale as a recurrent motif pervades in operatic tragedy; and when the main story is reached, we behold the modern Pyncheons in a pitiable state of decay. Poor old Hepzibah, the eccentric reduced gentlewoman; childlike, unfortunate Clifford, just released from undeserved imprisonment; sly and treacherous judge Pyncheon, who is the old Colonel all over again — all these figures are tremendous symbols, and are well matched by the stunted vegetation and anæmic fowls in the garden. It was almost a pity to supply a fairly happy ending, with a union of sprightly Phœbe, cousin and last scion of the Pyncheons, to the prepossessing young man who turns out to be the last of the Maules. This union, presumably, ends the curse. Hawthorne avoids all violence of diction or movement, and keeps his implications of terror well in the background; but occasional glimpses amply serve to sustain the mood and redeem the work from pure allegorical aridity. Incidents like the bewitching of Alice Pyncheon in the early eighteenth century, and the spectral music of her harpsichord which precedes a death in the family — the latter a variant of an immemorial type of Aryan myth — link the action directly with the supernatural; whilst the dead nocturnal vigil of old judge Pyncheon in the ancient parlour, with his frightfully ticking watch, is stark horror of the most poignant and genuine sort. The way in which the judge's death is first adumbrated by the motions and sniffing of a strange cat outside the window, long before the fact is suspected by the reader or by any of the characters, is a stroke of genius which Poe could not have surpassed. Later the strange cat watches intently outside that same window in the night and on the next day, for — something. It is clearly the psychopomp of primeval myth, fitted and adapted with infinite deftness to its latter-day setting.

But Hawthorne left no well-defined literary posterity. His mood and attitude belonged to the age which closed with him, and it is the spirit of Poe — who so clearly and realistically understood the natural basis of the horror-appeal and the correct mechanics of its achievement — which survived and blossomed. Among the earliest of Poe's disciples may be reckoned the brilliant young Irishman Fitz James O'Brien (1828-1862), who became naturalised as an American and perished honourably in the Civil War. It is he who gave us *What Was It?*, the first well-shaped short story of a tangible but invisible being, and the prototype of de Maupassant's *Horla;* he also who created the inimitable *Diamond Lens,* in which a young microscopist falls in love with a maiden of an infinitesimal world which he has discovered in a drop of water. O'Brien's early death undoubtedly deprived us of some masterful tales of strangeness and terror, though his genius was not, properly speaking, of the same titan quality which characterised Poe and Hawthorne.

Closer to real greatness was the eccentric and saturnine journalist Ambrose Bierce, born in 1842; who likewise entered the Civil War, but survived to write some immortal tales and to disappear in 1913 in as great a cloud of mystery as any he ever evoked from his nightmare fancy. Bierce was a satirist and pamphleteer of note, but the bulk of his artistic reputation must rest upon his grim and savage short stories; a large number of which deal with the Civil War and form the most vivid and realistic expression which that conflict has yet received in fiction. Virtually all of Bierce's tales are tales of horror; and whilst many of them treat only of the physical and psychological horrors within Nature, a substantial proportion admit the malignly supernatural and form a leading element in America's fund of weird literature. Mr. Samuel Loveman, a living poet and critic who was personally acquainted with Bierce, thus sums up the genius of the great "shadow-maker" in the preface to some of his letters:

> In Bierce the evocation of horror becomes for the first time not so much the prescription or perversion of Poe and Maupassant, but an atmosphere definite and uncannily precise. Words, so simple that one would be prone to ascribe them to the limitations of a literary hack, take on an unholy horror, a new and unguessed transformation. In Poe one finds it a *tour de force*, in Maupassant a nervous engagement of the flagellated climax. To Bierce, simply and sincerely, diabolism held in its tormented death a legitimate and reliant means to the end. Yet a tacit confirmation with Nature is in every instance insisted upon.
>
> In *The Death of Halpin Frayser* flowers, verdure, and the boughs and leaves of trees are magnificently placed as an opposing foil to unnatural malignity. Not the accustomed golden world, but a world pervaded with the mystery of blue and the breathless recalcitrance of dreams is Bierce's. Yet, curiously, inhumanity is not altogether absent.

The "inhumanity" mentioned by Mr. Loveman finds vent in a rare strain of sardonic comedy and graveyard humour, and a kind of delight in images of cruelty and tantalising disappointment. The former quality is well illustrated by some of the subtitles in the darker narratives; such as "One does not always eat what is on the table", describing a body laid out for a coroner's inquest, and "A man though naked may be in rags," referring to a frightfully mangled corpse.

Bierce's work is in general somewhat uneven. Many of the stories are obviously mechanical, and marred by a jaunty and commonplacely artificial style derived from journalistic models; but the grim malevolence stalking through all of them is unmistakable, and several stand out as permanent mountain-peaks of American weird writing. *The Death of Halpin Frayser*, called by Frederic Taber Cooper the most fiendishly ghastly tale in the literature of the Anglo-Saxon race, tells of a body skulking by night without a soul in a weird and horribly ensanguined wood, and of a man beset by ancestral memories who met death at the claws of that which had been his fervently loved mother. *The Damned Thing*, frequently copied in popular anthologies, chronicles the hideous devastations of an invisible entity that waddles and flounders on the hills and in the wheat-fields by night and day. *The Suitable Surroundings* evokes with singular subtlety yet apparent simplicity a piercing sense of the terror which may reside in the written word. In the story the weird author Colston says to his friend Marsh, "You are brave enough to read me in a street-car, but — in a deserted house — alone — in the forest — at night! Bah! I have a manuscript in my pocket that would kill you!" Marsh reads the manuscript in "the suitable surroundings" — and it does kill him. *The Middle Toe of the Right Foot* is clumsily developed, but has a powerful climax. A man named Manton has horribly killed his two children and his wife, the latter of whom lacked the middle toe of the right foot. Ten years later he returns much altered to the neighbourhood; and, being secretly recognised, is provoked into a bowie-knife duel in the dark, to be held in the now abandoned house where his crime was committed. When the moment of the duel arrives a trick is played upon him; and he is left without an antagonist, shut in a night-black ground floor room of the reputedly haunted edifice, with the thick dust of a decade on every hand. No knife is drawn against him, for only a thorough scare is intended; but on the next day he is found crouched in a corner with distorted face, dead of sheer fright at something he has seen. The only clue visible to the discoverers is one having terrible implications: "In the dust of years that lay thick upon the floor — leading from the door by which they had entered, straight across the room to within a yard of Manton's crouching corpse — were three parallel lines of footprints — light but definite impressions of bare feet, the outer ones those of small children, the inner a woman's. From the point at which they ended they did not return; they pointed all one way." And, of course, the woman's prints showed a lack of the middle toe of the right foot. *The Spook House*, told with a severely homely air of journalistic verisimilitude, conveys terrible hints of shocking mystery. In 1858 an entire family of seven persons disappears suddenly and unaccountably from a plantation house in eastern Kentucky, leaving all its possessions untouched — furniture, clothing, food supplies, horses, cattle, and slaves. About a year later two men of high standing are forced by a storm to take shelter in the deserted dwelling, and in so doing stumble into a strange subterranean room lit by an unaccountable greenish light and having an iron door which cannot be opened from within. In this room lie the decayed corpses of all the missing family; and as one of the discoverers rushes forward to embrace a body he seems to recognise, the other is so overpowered by a strange foetor that he accidentally shuts his companion in the vault and loses consciousness. Recovering his senses six weeks later, the survivor is unable to find the hidden room; and the house is burned during the Civil War. The imprisoned discoverer is never seen or heard of again.

Bierce seldom realises the atmospheric possibilities of his themes as vividly as Poe; and much of his work contains a certain touch of naïveté, prosaic angularity, or early-American provincialism which contrasts somewhat with the efforts of later horror-masters. Nevertheless the genuineness and artistry of his dark intimations are always unmistakable, so that his greatness is in no danger of eclipse. As arranged in his definitively collected works, Bierce's weird tales occur mainly in two volumes, *Can Such Things Be?* and *In the Midst of Life.* The former, indeed, is almost wholly given over to the supernatural.

Much of the best in American horror-literature has come from pens not mainly devoted to that medium. Oliver Wendell Holmes's historic *Elsie Venner* suggests with admirable restraint an unnatural ophidian element in a young woman prenatally influenced, and sustains the atmosphere with finely discriminating landscape touches. In *The Turn of the Screw,* Henry James triumphs over his inevitable pomposity and prolixity sufficiently well to create a truly potent air of sinister menace; depicting the hideous influence of two dead and evil servants, Peter Quint and the governess, Miss Jessel, over a small boy and girl who had been under their care. James is perhaps too diffuse, too unctuously urbane, and too much addicted to subtleties of speech to realise fully all the wild and devastating horror in his situations; but for all that there is a rare and mounting tide of fright, culminating in the death of the little boy, which gives the novelette a permanent place in its special class.

F. Marion Crawford produced several weird tales of varying quality, now collected in a volume entitled *Wandering Ghosts*. *For the Blood Is the Life* touches powerfully on a case of moon-cursed vampirism near an ancient tower on the rocks of the lonely South Italian seacoast. *The Dead Smile* treats of family horrors in an old house and an ancestral vault in Ireland, and introduces the banshee with considerable force. *The Upper Berth*, however, is Crawford's weird masterpiece; and is one of the most tremendous horror-stories in all literature. In this tale of a suicide-haunted stateroom such things as the spectral saltwater dampness, the strangely open porthole, and the nightmare struggle with the nameless object are handled with incomparable dexterity.

Very genuine, though not without the typical mannered extravagance of the eighteen-nineties, is the strain of horror in the early work of Robert W. Chambers, since renowned for products of a very different quality. *The King in Yellow*, a series of vaguely connected short stories having as a background a monstrous and suppressed book whose perusal brings fright, madness, and spectral tragedy, really achieves notable heights of cosmic fear in spite of uneven interest and a somewhat trivial and affected cultivation of the Gallic studio atmosphere made popular by Du Maurier's *Trilby*. The most powerful of its tales, perhaps, is *The Yellow Sign*, in which is introduced a silent and terrible churchyard watchman with a face like a puffy grave-worm's. A boy, describing a tussle he has had with this creature, shivers and sickens as he relates a certain detail. "Well, it's Gawd's truth that when I 'it 'im 'e grabbed me wrists, Sir, and when I twisted 'is soft, mushy fist one of 'is fingers come off in me 'and." An artist, who after seeing him has shared with another a strange dream of a nocturnal hearse, is shocked by the voice with which the watchman accosts him. The fellow emits a muttering sound that fills the head "like thick oily smoke from a fat-rendering vat or an odour of noisome decay." What he mumbles is merely this: "Have you found the Yellow Sign?"

A weirdly hieroglyphed onyx talisman, picked up on the street by the sharer of his dream, is shortly given the artist; and after stumbling queerly upon the hellish and forbidden book of horrors the two learn, among other hideous things which no sane mortal should know, that this talisman is indeed the nameless Yellow Sign handed down from the accursed cult of Hastur — from primordial Carcosa, whereof the volume treats, and some nightmare memory of which seeks to lurk latent and ominous at the back of all men's minds. Soon they hear the rumbling of the black-plumed hearse driven by the flabby and corpse-faced watchman. He enters the night-shrouded house in quest of the Yellow Sign, all bolts and bars rotting at his touch. And when the people rush in, drawn by a scream that no human throat could utter, they find three forms on the floor — two dead and one dying. One of the dead shapes is far gone in decay. It is the churchyard watchman, and the doctor exclaims, "That man must have been dead for months." It is worth observing that the author derives most of the names and allusions connected with his eldritch land of primal memory from the tales of Ambrose Bierce. Other early works of Mr. Chambers displaying the outré and macabre element are *The Maker of Moons* and *In Search of the Unknown*. One cannot help regretting that he did not further develop a vein in which he could so easily have become a recognised master.

Horror material of authentic force may be found in the work of the New England realist Mary E. Wilkins, whose volume of short tales, *The Wind in the Rosebush,* contains a number of noteworthy achievements. In *The Shadows on the Wall* we are shown with consummate skill the response of a staid New England household to uncanny tragedy; and the sourceless shadow of the poisoned brother well prepares us for the climactic moment when the shadow of the secret murderer, who has killed himself in a neighbouring city, suddenly appears beside it. Charlotte Perkins Gilman, in *The Yellow Wall Paper,* rises to a classic level in subtly delineating the madness which crawls over a woman dwelling in the hideously papered room where a madwoman was once confined.

In *The Dead Valley* the eminent architect and mediævalist Ralph Adams Cram achieves a memorably potent degree of vague regional horror through subtleties of atmosphere and description.

Still further carrying on our spectral tradition is the gifted and versatile humourist Irvin S. Cobb, whose work both early and recent contains some finely weird specimens. *Fishhead,* an early achievement, is banefully effective in its

portrayal of unnatural affinities between a hybrid idiot and
the strange fish of an isolated lake, which at the last avenge
their biped kinsman's murder. Later work of Mr. Cobb introduces an element of possible science, as in the tale of hereditary memory where a modern man with a negroid strain
utters words in African jungle speech when run down by a
train under visual and aural circumstances recalling the
maiming of his black ancestor by a rhinoceros a century
before.

Extremely high in artistic stature is the novel *The Dark
Chamber* (1927) by the late Leonard Cline. This is the tale of a
man who — with the characteristic ambition of the Gothic or
Byronic hero-villain — seeks to defy nature and recapture
every moment of his past life through the abnormal stimulation of memory. To this end he employs endless notes,
records, mnemonic objects, and pictures — and finally
odours, music, and exotic drugs. At last his ambition goes
beyond his personal life and readies toward the black
abysses of *hereditary* memory — even back to pre-human
days amidst the steaming swamps of the carboniferous age,
and to still more unimaginable deeps of primal time and
entity. He calls for madder music and takes stranger drugs,
and finally his great dog grows oddly afraid of him. A noxious animal stench encompasses him, and he grows vacant-
faced and subhuman. In the end he takes to the woods,
howling at night beneath windows. He is finally found in a
thicket, mangled to death. Beside him is the mangled corpse
of his dog. They have killed each other. The atmosphere of
this novel is malevolently potent, much attention being paid
to the central figure's sinister home and household.

A less subtle and well-balanced but nevertheless highly

effective creation is Herbert S. Gorman's novel, *The Place Called Dagon,* which relates the dark history of a western Massachusetts back-water where the descendants of refugees from the Salem witchcraft still keep alive the morbid and degenerate horrors of the Black Sabbat.

Sinister House, by Leland Hall, has touches of magnificent atmosphere but is marred by a somewhat mediocre romanticism.

Very notable in their way are some of the weird conceptions of the novelist and short-story writer Edward Lucas White, most of whose themes arise from actual dreams. *The Song of The Siren* has a very persuasive strangeness, while such things as *Lukundoo* and *The Snout* arouse darker apprehensions. Mr. White imparts a very peculiar quality to his tales — an oblique sort of glamour which has its own distinctive type of convincingness.

Of younger Americans, none strikes the note of cosmic horror so well as the California poet, artist and fictionist Clark Ashton Smith, whose bizarre writing, drawings, paintings and stories are the delight of a sensitive few. Mr. Smith has for his background a universe of remote and paralysing fright-jungles of poisonous and iridescent blossoms on the moons of Saturn, evil and grotesque temples in Atlantis, Lemuria, and forgotten elder worlds, and dank morasses of spotted death-fungi in spectral countries beyond earth's rim. His longest and most ambitious poem, *The Hashish-Eater,* is in pentameter blank verse; and opens up chaotic and incredible vistas of kaleidoscopic nightmare in the spaces between the stars. In sheer dæmonic strangeness and fertility of conception, Mr. Smith is perhaps unexcelled by, any, other writer dead or living. Who else has seen such gorgeous, luxuriant, and feverishly distorted visions of infinite spheres and multiple dimensions and lived to tell the tale? His short stories deal powerfully with other galaxies, worlds, and dimensions, as well as with strange regions and æons on the earth. He tells of primal Hyperborea and its black amorphous god Tsathoggua; of the lost continent Zothique, and of the fabulous, Vampire-curst land of Averoigne in mediæval France. Some of Mr. Smith's best work can be found in the brochure entitled *The Double Shadow and Other Fantasies* (1933).

IX.

The Weird Tradition in the British Isles

RECENT British literature, besides including the three or four greatest fantaisistes of the present age, has been gratifyingly fertile in the element of the weird. Rudyard Kipling has often approached it, and has, despite the omnipresent mannerisms, handled it with indubitable mastery in such tales as *The Phantom Rickshaw, The Finest Story in the World, The Recrudescence of Imray,* and *The Mark of the Beast.* This latter is of particular poignancy; the pictures of the naked leper-priest who mewed like an otter, of the spots which appeared on the chest of the man that priest cursed, of the growing carnivorousness of the victim and of the fear which horses began to display toward him, and of the eventually half-accomplished transformation of that victim into a leopard, being things which no reader is ever likely to forget. The final defeat of the malignant sorcery does not impair the force of the tale or the validity of its mystery.

Lafcadio Hearn, strange, wandering, and exotic, de-

SUPERNATURAL HORROR IN LITERATURE ∞ 81

parts still farther from the realm of the real; and with the supreme artistry of a sensitive poet weaves phantasies impossible to an author of the solid roast beef type. His *Fantastics*, written in America, contains some of the most impressive ghoulishness in all literature; whilst his *Kwaidan*, written in Japan, crystallises with matchless skill and delicacy the eerie lore and whispered legends of that richly colourful nation. Still more of Hearn's wizardry of language is shown in some of his translations from the French, especially from Gautier and Flaubert. His version of the latter's *Temptation of St. Anthony* is a classic of fevered and riotous imagery clad in the magic of singing words.

Oscar Wilde may likewise be given a place amongst weird writers, both for certain of his exquisite fairy tales, and for his vivid *Picture of Dorian Gray*, in which a marvellous portrait for years assumes the duty of aging and coarsening instead of its original, who meanwhile plunges into every excess of vice and crime without the outward loss of youth, beauty, and freshness. There is a sudden and potent climax when Dorian Gray, at last become a murderer, seeks to destroy the painting whose changes testify to his moral degeneracy. He stabs it with a knife, and a hideous cry and crash are heard; but when the servants enter they find it in all its pristine loveliness. "Lying on the floor was a dead man, in evening dress, with a knife in his heart. He was withered, wrinkled, and loathsome of visage. It was not until they had examined the rings that they recognised who he was."

Matthew Phipps Shiel, author of many weird, grotesque, and adventurous novels and tales, occasionally attains a high level of horrific magic. *Xelucha* is a noxiously hideous fragment, but is excelled by Mr. Shiel's undoubted masterpiece, *The House of Sounds*, floridly written in the "yellow nineties," and recast with more artistic restraint in the early twentieth century. This story, in final form, deserves a place among the foremost things of its kind. It tells of a creeping horror and menace trickling down the centuries on a sub-arctic island off the coast of Norway; where, amidst the sweep of dæmon winds and the ceaseless din of hellish waves and cataracts, a vengeful dead man built a brazen tower of terror. It is vaguely like, yet infinitely unlike, Poe's *Fall of the House of Usher*. In the novel *The Purple Cloud* Mr. Shiel describes with tremendous power a curse which came out of the arctic to destroy mankind, and which for a time appears to have left but a single inhabitant on our planet. The sensations of this lone survivor as he realises his position, and roams through the corpse-littered and treasure-strewn cities of the world as their absolute master, are delivered with a skill and artistry falling little short of actual majesty. Unfortunately the second half of the book, with its conventionally romantic element, involves a distinct letdown.

Better known than Shiel is the ingenious Bram Stoker, who created many starkly horrific conceptions in a series of novels whose poor technique sadly impairs their net effect. *The Lair of the White Worm*, dealing with a gigantic primitive entity that lurks in a vault beneath an ancient castle, utterly ruins a magnificent idea by a development almost infantile. *The Jewel of Seven Stars*, touching on a strange Egyptian resurrection, is less crudely written. But best of all is the famous *Dracula*, which has become almost the standard modern exploitation of the frightful vampire myth. Count Dracula, a vampire, dwells in a horrible castle in the Carpathians, but finally migrates to England with the design of populating the country with fellow vampires. How an Englishman fares within Dracula's stronghold of terrors, and how the dead fiend's plot for domination is at last defeated, are elements which unite to form a tale now justly assigned a permanent place in English letters. *Dracula* evoked many similar novels of supernatural horror, among which the best are perhaps *The Beetle*, by Richard Marsh, *Brood of the Witch-Queen*, by "Sax Rohmer" (Arthur Sarsfield Ward), and *The Door of the Unreal*, by Gerald Bliss. The latter handles quite dexterously the standard werewolf superstition. Much subtler and more artistic, and told with singular skill through the juxtaposed narratives of the several characters, is the novel *Cold Harbour*, by Francis Brett Young, in which an ancient house of strange malignancy is powerfully delineated. The mocking and well-nigh omnipotent fiend Humphrey Furnival holds echoes of the Manfred-Montoni type of early Gothic "villain," but is redeemed from triteness by many clever individualities. Only the slight diffuseness of explanation at the close, and the somewhat too free use of divination as a plot factor, keep this tale from approaching absolute perfection.

In the novel *Witch Wood* John Buchan depicts with tremendous force a survival of the evil Sabbat in a lonely district of Scotland. The description of the black forest with the evil stone, and of the terrible cosmic adumbrations when the horror is finally extirpated, will repay one for wading through the very gradual action and plethora of Scottish dialect. Some of Mr. Buchan's short stories are also extremely vivid in their spectral intimations; *The Green Wildebeest*, a tale of African witchcraft, *The Wind in the Portico,* with its awakening of dead Britanno-Roman horrors, and *Skule Skerry,* with its touches of sub-arctic fright, being especially remarkable.

Clemence Housman, in the brief novelette *The Werewolf,* attains a high degree of gruesome tension and achieves to some extent the atmosphere of authentic folklore. In *The Elixir of Life* Arthur Ransome attains some darkly excellent effects despite a general naïveté of plot, while H. B. Drake's *The Shadowy Thing* summons up strange and terrible vistas. George Macdonald's *Lilith* has a compelling bizarrerie all its own, the first and simpler of the two versions being perhaps the more effective.

Deserving of distinguished notice as a forceful craftsman to whom an unseen mystic world is ever a close and vital reality is the poet Walter de la Mare, whose haunting verse and exquisite prose alike bear consistent traces of a strange vision reaching deeply into veiled spheres of beauty and terrible and forbidden dimensions of being. In the novel *The Return* we see the soul of a dead man reach out of its grave of two centuries and fasten itself upon the flesh of the living, so that even the face of the victim becomes that which had long ago returned to dust. Of the shorter tales, of which several volumes exist, many are unforgettable for their command of fear's and sorcery's darkest ramifications; notably *Seaton's Aunt,* in which there lowers a noxious background of malignant vampirism; *The Tree,* which tells of a frightful vegetable growth in the yard of a starving artist; *Out of the Deep,* wherein we are given leave to imagine what thing answered the summons of a dying wastrel in a dark lonely house when he pulled a long-feared bell-cord in the attic of his dread-haunted boyhood; *A Recluse,* which hints at what sent a chance guest flying from a house in the night; *Mr. Kempe,* which shows us a mad clerical hermit in quest of the human soul, dwelling in a frightful sea-cliff region beside an archaic abandoned chapel; and *All-Hallows,* a glimpse of dæmoniac forces besieging a lonely mediæval church and miraculously restoring the rotting masonry. De la Mare does not make fear the sole or even the dominant element of most of his tales, being apparently more interested in the subtleties of character involved. Occasionally he sinks to sheer whimsical phantasy of the Barrie order. Still he is among the very few to whom unreality is a vivid, living presence; and as such he is able to put into his occasional fear-studies a keen potency which only a rare master can achieve. His poem *The Listeners* restores the Gothic shudder to modern verse.

The weird short story has fared well of late, an important contributor being the versatile E. F. Benson, whose *The Man Who Went Too Far* breathes whisperingly of a house at the edge of a dark wood, and of Pan's hoof-mark on the breast of a dead man. Mr. Benson's volume, *Visible and Invisible,* contains several stories of singular power; notably *Negotiam Perambulans,* whose unfolding reveals an abnormal monster from an ancient ecclesiastical panel which performs an act of miraculous vengeance in a lonely village on the Cornish coast, and *The Horror-Horn,* through which lopes a terrible half-human survival dwelling on unvisited Alpine peaks. *The Face,* in another collection, is lethally potent, in its relentless aura of doom. H. R. Wakefield, in his collections, *They Return at Evening* and *Others Who Return,* manages now and then to achieve great heights of horror despite a vitiating air of sophistication. The most notable stories are *The Red Lodge* with its slimy acqueous evil, *He Cometh and He Passeth By, And He Shall Sing, The Cairn,Look Up There,Blind Man's Buff,* and that bit of lurking millennial horror, *The Seventeenth Hole at Duncaster.* Mention has been made of the weird work of H.G. Wells and A. Conan Doyle. The former, in *The Ghost of Fear,* reaches a very high level while all the items in *Thirty Strange Stories* have strong fantastic implications. Doyle now and then struck a powerfully spectral note, as in *The Captain of the Pole-Star,* a tale of arctic ghostliness, and *Lot No. 249,* wherein the reanimated mummy theme is used with more than ordinary skill. Hugh Walpole, of the same family as the founder of Gothic fiction, has sometimes approached the bizarre with much success, his short story *Mrs. Lunt* carrying a very poignant shudder. John Metcalfe, in the collection published as *The Smoking Leg,* attains now and then a rare pitch of potency, the tale entitled *The Bad Lands,* containing graduations of horror that strongly savour of genius. More whimiscial and inclined toward the amiable and innocuous phantasy of Sir J. M. Barrie are the short tales of E.M. Forster, grouped under the title of *The Celestial Omnibus.* Of these only one, dealing with a glimpse of Pan and his aura of fright, may be said to hold the true element of cosmic horror. Mrs. H.D. Everett, though adhering to very old and conventional models, occasionally reaches singular heights of spiritual terror in her collection of short stories, *The Death Mask.* L. P. Hartley is notable for his incisive and extremely ghastly tale, *A Visitor from Down Under,* May Sinclair's *Uncanny Stories* contain more of traditional "occultism" than of that creative treatment of fear which marks mastery in this field, and are inclined to lay more stress on human emotions and psychological delving than upon the stark phenomena of a cosmos utterly unreal. It may be well to remark here that occult believers are probably less effective than materialists in delineating the spectral and the fantastic, since to them the phantom world is so commonplace a reality that they tend to refer to it with less awe, remoteness, and impressiveness than do those who see in it an absolute and stupendous violation of the natural order.

Of rather uneven stylistic quality, but vast occasional power in its suggestion of lurking worlds and beings behind the ordinary surface of life, is the work of William Hope Hodgson, known today far less than it deserves to be. Despite a tendency toward conventionally sentimental conceptions of the universe, and of man's relation to it and to his fellows, Mr. Hodgson is perhaps second only to Algernon Blackwood in his serious treatment of unreality. Few can equal him in adumbrating the nearness of nameless forces and monstrous besieging entities through casual hints and insignificant details, or in conveying feelings of the spectral and the abnormal in connection with regions or buildings.

In *The Boats of the Glen Carrig* (1907) we are shown a variety of malign marvels and accursed unknown lands as encountered by the survivors of a sunken ship. The brooding menace in the earlier parts of the book is impossible to surpass, though a letdown in the direction of ordinary romance and adventure occurs toward the end. An inaccurate and pseudo-romantic attempt to reproduce eighteenth-century prose detracts from the general effect, but the really profound nautical erudition everywhere displayed is a compensating factor.

The House on the Borderland (1908) — perhaps the greatest of all Mr. Hodgson's works — tells of a lonely and evilly regarded house in Ireland which forms a focus for hideous otherworld forces and sustains a siege by blasphemous hybrid anomalies from a hidden abyss below. The wanderings of the Narrator's spirit through limitless light-years of cosmic space and Kalpas of eternity, and its witnessing of the solar system's final destruction, constitute something almost unique in standard literature. And everywhere there is manifest the author's power to suggest vague, ambushed horrors in natural scenery. But for a few touches of commonplace sentimentality this book would be a classic of the first water.

The Ghost Pirates (1909), regarded by Mr. Hodgson as rounding out a trilogy with the two previously mentioned works, is a powerful account of a doomed and haunted ship on its last voyage, and of the terrible sea-devils (of quasi-human aspect, and perhaps the spirits of bygone buccaneers) that besiege it and finally drag it down to an unknown fate. With its command of maritime knowledge, and its clever selection of hints and incidents suggestive of latent horrors in nature, this book at times reaches enviable peaks of power.

The Night Land (1912) is a long-extended (538 pp.) tale of the earth's infinitely remote future—billions and billions of years ahead, after the death of the sun. It is told in a rather clumsy fashion, as the dreams of a man in the seventeenth century, whose mind merges with its own future incarnation; and is seriously marred by painful verboseness, repetitiousness, artificial and nauseously sticky romantic sentimentality, and an attempt at archaic language even more grotesque and absurd than that in *Glen Carrig*.

Allowing for all its faults, it is yet one of the most potent pieces of macabre imagination ever written. The picture of a night-black, dead planet, with the remains of the human race concentrated in a stupendously vast mental pyramid and besieged by monstrous, hybrid, and altogether unknown forces of the darkness, is something that no reader can ever forget: Shapes and entities of an altogether non-human and inconceivable sort — the prowlers of the black, man-forsaken, and unexplored world outside the pyramid — are suggested and partly described with ineffable potency; while the night-land landscape with its chasms and slopes and dying volcanism takes on an almost sentient terror beneath the author's touch.

Midway in the book the central figure ventures outside the pyramid on a quest through death-haunted realms untrod by man for millions of years — and in his slow, minutely described, day-by-day progress over unthinkable leagues of immemorial blackness there is a sense of cosmic alienage, breathless mystery, and terrified expectancy unrivalled in the whole range of literature. The last quarter of the book drags woefully, but fails to spoil the tremendous power of the whole. Mr. Hodgson's later volume, *Carnacki, the Ghost-Finder*, consists of several longish short stories published many years before in magazines. In quality it falls conspicuously below the level of the other books. We here find a more or less conventional stock figure of the "infallible detective" type — the progeny of M. Dupin and Sherlock Holmes, and the close kin of Algernon Blackwood's John Silence — moving through scenes and events badly marred by an atmosphere of professional "occultism." A few of the episodes, however, are of undeniable power, and afford glimpses of the peculiar genius characteristic of the author.

Naturally it is impossible in brief sketch to trace out all the classic modern uses of the terror element. The ingredient must of necessity enter into all work, both prose and verse, treating broadly of life; and we are therefore not surprised to find a share in such writers as the poet Browning, whose *Childe Roland to the Dark Tower Came* is instinct with hideous menace, or the novelist Joseph Conrad, who often wrote of the dark secrets within the sea, and of the dæmoniac driving power of Fate as influencing the lives of lonely and maniacally resolute men. Its trail is one of infinite ramifications; but we must here confine ourselves to its appearance in a relatively unmixed state, where it determines and dominates the work of art containing it.

Somewhat separate from the main British stream is that current of weirdness in Irish literature which came to the fore in the Celtic Renaissance of the later nineteenth and early twentieth centuries. Ghost and fairy lore have always been of great prominence in Ireland, and for over a hundred years have been recorded by a line of such faithful transcribers and translators as William Carleton, T. Crofton Croker, Lady Wilde — mother of Oscar Wilde — Douglas Hyde, and W.B. Yeats. Brought to notice by the modern movement, this body of myth has been carefully collected and studied; and its salient features reproduced in the work of later figures like Yeats, J. M. Synge, "A. E.," Lady Gregory, Padraic Colum, James Stephens and their colleagues.

Whilst on the whole more whimsically fantastic than terrible, such folklore and its consciously artistic counterparts contain much that falls truly within the domain of cosmic horror. Tales of burials in sunken churches beneath haunted lakes, accounts of death-heralding banshees and sinister changelings, ballads of spectres and "the unholy creatures of the Raths" — all these have their poignant and definite shivers, and mark a strong and distinctive element in weird literature. Despite homely grotesqueness and absolute naïveté, there is genuine nightmare in the class of narrative represented by the yarn of Teig O'Kane, who in punishment for his wild life was ridden all night by a hideous corpse that demanded burial and drove him from churchyard to churchyard as the dead rose up loathsomely in each one and refused to accommodate the newcomer with a berth. Yeats, undoubtedly the greatest figure of the Irish revival if not the greatest of all living poets, has accomplished notable things both in original work and in the codification of old legends.

X.

The Modern Masters

THE best horror-tales of today, profiting by the long evolution of the type, possess a naturalness, convincingness, artistic smoothness, and skilful intensity of appeal quite beyond comparison with anything in the Gothic work of a century or more ago. Technique, craftsmanship, experience, and psychological knowledge have advanced tremendously with the passing years, so that much of the older work seems naïve and artificial; redeemed, when redeemed at all, only by a genius which conquers heavy limitations. The tone of jaunty and inflated romance, full of false motivation and investing every conceivable event with a counterfeit significance and carelessly inclusive glamour, is now confined to lighter and more whimiscal phases of supernatural writing. Serious weird stories are either made realistically intense by close consistency and perfect fidelity to Nature except in the one supernatural direction which the author allows himself, or else cast altogether in the realm of phantasy, with atmosphere cunningly adapted to the visualisation of a delicately exotic world of unreality beyond space and time, in which almost anything may happen if it but happen in true accord with certain types of imagination and illusion normal to the sensitive human brain. This, at least, is the dominant tendency; though of course many great contemporary writers slip occasionally into some of the flashy postures of immature romanticism or into bits of the equally empty and absurd jargon of pseudo-scientific "occultism," now at one of its periodic high tides.

Of living creators of cosmic fear raised to its most artistic pitch, few if any can hope to equal the versatile Arthur Machen, author of some dozen tales long and short, in which the elements of hidden horror and brooding fright attain an almost incomparable substance and realistic acuteness. Mr. Machen, a general man of letters and master of an exquisitely lyrical and expressive prose style, has perhaps put more conscious effort into his picaresque Chronicles of Clemendy, his refreshing essays, his vivid autobiographical volumes, his fresh and spirited translations, and above all his memorable epic of the sensitive æsthetic mind, *The Hill of Dreams*, in which the youthful hero responds to the magic of that ancient Welsh environment which is the author's own, and lives a dream-life in the Roman city of Isca Silurum, now shrunk to the relic-strown village of Caerleon-on-Usk. But the fact remains that his powerful horror-material of the nineties and earlier nineteen-hundreds stands alone in its class, and marks a distinct epoch in the history of this literary form.

Mr. Machen, with an impressionable Celtic heritage linked to keen youthful memories of the wild domed hills, archaic forests, and cryptical Roman ruins of the Gwent countryside, has developed an imaginative life of rare beauty, intensity, and historic background. He has absorbed the mediæval mystery of dark woods and ancient customs, and is a champion of the Middle Ages in all things — including the Catholic faith. He has yielded, likewise, to the spell of the Britanno-Roman life which once surged over his native region; and finds strange magic in the fortified camps, tessellated pavements, fragments of statues, and kindred things which tell of the day when classicism reigned and Latin was the language of the country. A young American poet, Frank Belknap Long, has well summarised this dreamer's rich endowments and wizardry of expression in the sonnet "On Reading Arthur Machen":

> There is a glory in the autumn wood,
> The ancient lanes of England wind and climb
> Past wizard oaks and gorse and tangled thyme
> To where a fort of mighty empire stood:
> There is a glamour in the autumn sky;
> The reddened clouds are writhing in the glow
> Of some great fire, and there are glints below
> Of tawny yellow where the embers die.
> I wait, for he will show me, clear and cold,
> High-rais'd in splendour, sharp against the North,

The Roman eagles, and through mists of gold
The marching legions as they issue forth:
I wait, for I would share with him again
The ancient wisdom, and the ancient pain.

Of Mr. Machen's horror-tales the most famous is perhaps *The Great God Pan* (1894) which tells of a singular and
terrible experiment and its consequences. A young woman,
through surgery of the brain-cells, is made to see the vast
and monstrous deity of Nature, and becomes an idiot in con-
sequence, dying less than a year later. Years afterward a
strange, ominous, and foreign-looking child named Helen
Vaughan is placed to board with a family in rural Wales, and
haunts the woods in unaccountable fashion. A little boy is
thrown out of his mind at sight of someone or something he
spies with her, and a young girl comes to a terrible end in
similar fashion. All this mystery is strangely interwoven
with the Roman rural deities of the place, as sculptured in
antique fragments. After another lapse of years, a woman of
strangely exotic beauty appears in society, drives her husband to horror and death, causes an artist to paint unthinkable paintings of Witches' Sabbaths, creates an epidemic of
suicide among the men of her acquaintance, and is finally
discovered to be a frequenter of the lowest dens of vice in
London, where even the most callous degenerates are
shocked at her enormities. Through the clever comparing of
notes on the part of those who have had word of her at various stages of her career, this woman is discovered to be the
girl Helen Vaughan, who is the child — by no mortal
father — of the young woman on whom the brain experiment was made. She is a daughter of hideous Pan himself,
and at the last is put to death amidst horrible transmutations

of form involving changes of sex and a descent to the most primal manifestations of the life-principle.

But the charm of the tale is in the telling. No one could begin to describe the cumulative suspense and ultimate horror with which every paragraph abounds without following fully the precise order in which Mr. Machen unfolds his gradual hints and revelations. Melodrama is undeniably present, and coincidence is stretched to a length which appears absurd upon analysis; but in the malign witchery of the tale as a whole these trifles are forgotten, and the sensitive reader reaches the end with only an appreciative shudder and a tendency to repeat the words of one of the characters: "It is too incredible, too monstrous; such things can never be in this quiet world. . . . Why, man, if such a case were possible, our earth would be a nightmare."

Less famous and less complex in plot than *The Great God Pan*, but definitely finer in atmosphere and general artistic value, is the curious and dimly disquieting chronicle called *The White People*, whose central portion purports to be the diary or notes of a little girl whose nurse has introduced her to some of the forbidden magic and soul-blasting traditions of the noxious witch-cult — the cult whose whispered lore was handed down long lines of peasantry throughout Western Europe, and whose members sometimes stole forth at night, one by one, to meet in black woods and lonely places for the revolting orgies of the Witches' Sabbath. Mr. Machen's narrative, a triumph of skilful selectiveness and restraint, accumulates enormous power as it flows on in a stream of innocent childish prattle, introducing allusions to strange "nymphs," "Dols," "voolas," "white, green, and scarlet ceremonies," "Aklo letters," "Chian language,"

"Mao games," and the like. The rites learned by the nurse from her witch grandmother are taught to the child by the time she is three years old, and her artless accounts of the dangerous secret revelations possess a lurking terror generously mixed with pathos. Evil charms well known to anthropologists are described with juvenile naïveté, and finally there comes a winter afternoon journey into the old Welsh hills, performed under an imaginative spell which lends to the wild scenery an added weirdness, strangeness, and suggestion of grotesque sentience. The details of this journey are given with marvellous vividness, and form to the keen critic a masterpiece of fantastic writing, with almost unlimited power in the intimation of potent hideousness and cosmic aberration. At length the child — whose age is then thirteen — comes upon a cryptic and banefully beautiful thing in the midst of a dark and inaccessible wood. In the end horror overtakes her in a manner deftly prefigured by an anecdote in the prologue, but she poisons herself in time. Like the mother of Helen Vaughan in *The Great God Pan*, she has seen that frightful deity. She is discovered dead in the dark wood beside the cryptic thing she found; and that thing — a whitely luminous statue of Roman workmanship about which dire mediæval rumours had clustered — is affrightedly hammered into dust by the searchers.

In the episodic novel of *The Three Impostors*, a work whose merit as a whole is somewhat marred by an imitation of the jaunty Stevenson manner, occur certain tales which perhaps represent the highwater mark of Machen's skill as a terror-weaver. Here we find in its most artistic form a favourite weird conception of the author's; the notion that beneath the mounds and rocks of the wild Welsh hills dwell subterraneously that squat primitive race whose vestiges gave rise to our common folk legends of fairies, elves, and the "little people," and whose acts are even now responsible for certain unexplained disappearances, and occasional substitutions of strange dark "changelings" for normal infants. This theme receives its finest treatment in the episode entitled *The Novel of the Black Seal*; where a professor, having discovered a singular identity between certain characters scrawled on Welsh limestone rocks and those existing in a prehistoric black seal from Babylon, sets out on a course of discovery which leads him to unknown and terrible things. A queer passage in the ancient geographer Solinus, a series of mysterious disappearances in the lonely reaches of Wales, a strange idiot son born to a rural mother after a fright in which her inmost faculties were shaken; all these things suggest to the professor a hideous connection and a condition revolting to any friend and respecter of the human race. He hires the idiot boy, who jabbers strangely at times in a repulsive hissing voice, and is subject to odd epileptic seizures. Once, after such a seizure in the professor's study by night, disquieting odours and evidences of unnatural presences are found; and soon after that the professor leaves a bulky document and goes into the weird hills with feverish expectancy and strange terror in his heart. He never returns, but beside a fantastic stone in the wild country are found his watch, money, and ring, done up with catgut in a parchment bearing the same terrible characters as those on the black Babylonish seal and the rock in the Welsh mountains.

The bulky document explains enough to bring up the most hideous vistas. Professor Gregg, from the massed evidence presented by the Welsh disappearances, the rock inscription, the accounts of ancient geographers, and the black seal, has decided that a frightful race of dark primal beings of immemorial antiquity and wide former diffusion still dwell beneath the hills of unfrequented Wales. Further research has unriddled the message of the black seal, and proved that the idiot boy, a son of some father more terrible than mankind, is the heir of monstrous memories and possibilities. That strange night in the study the professor invoked "the awful transmutation of the hills" by the aid of the black seal, and aroused in the hybrid idiot the horrors of his shocking paternity. He "saw his body swell and become distended as a bladder, while the face blackened. . . ." And then the supreme effects of the invocation appeared, and Professor Gregg knew the stark frenzy of cosmic panic in its darkest form. He knew the abysmal gulfs of abnormality that he had opened, and went forth into the wild hills prepared and resigned. He would meet the unthinkable "Little People" — and his document ends with a rational observation: "If unhappily I do not return from my journey, there is no need to conjure up here a picture of the awfulness of my fate."

Also in *The Three Impostors* is the *Novel of the White Powder*, which approaches the absolute culmination of loathsome fright. Francis Leicester, a young law student nervously worn out by seclusion and overwork, has a prescription filled by an old apothecary none too careful about the state of his drugs. The substance, it later turns out, is an unusual salt which time and varying temperature have accidentally changed to something very strange and terrible; nothing less, in short, than the mediæval vinum sabbati, whose consumption at the horrible orgies of the Witches'

Sabbath gave rise to shocking transformations and — if injudiciously used — to unutterable consequences. Innocently enough, the youth regularly imbibes the powder in a glass of water after meals; and at first seems substantially benefited. Gradually, however, his improved spirits take the form of dissipation; he is absent from home a great deal, and appears to have undergone a repellent psychological change. One day an odd livid spot appears on his right hand, and he afterward returns to his seclusion; finally keeping himself shut within his room and admitting none of the household. The doctor calls for an interview, and departs in a palsy of horror, saying that he can do no more in that house. Two weeks later the patient's sister, walking outside, sees a monstrous thing at the sickroom window; and servants report that food left at the locked door is no longer touched. Summons at the door bring only a sound of shuffling and a demand in a thick gurgling voice to be let alone. At last an awful happening is reported by a shuddering housemaid. The ceiling of the room below Leicester's is stained with a hideous black fluid, and a pool of viscid abomination has dripped to the bed beneath. Dr. Haberden, now persuaded to return to the house, breaks down the young man's door and strikes again and again with an iron bar at the blasphemous semiliving thing he finds there. It is "a dark and putrid mass, seething with corruption and hideous rottenness, neither liquid nor solid, but melting and changing." Burning points like eyes shine out of its midst, and before it is dispatched it tries to lift what might have been an arm. Soon afterward the physician, unable to endure the memory of what he has beheld, dies at sea while bound for a new life in America.

Mr. Machen returns to the dæmoniac "Little People" in *The Red Hand* and *The Shining Pyramid*; and in *The Terror*, a wartime story, he treats with very potent mystery the effect of man's modern repudiation of spirituality on the beasts of the world, which are thus led to question his supremacy and to unite for his extermination. Of utmost delicacy, and passing from mere horror into true mysticism, is *The Great Return*, a story of the Graal, also a product of the war period. Too well known to need description here is the tale of *The Bowmen*; which, taken for authentic narration, gave rise to the widespread legend of the "Angels of Mons" — ghosts of the old English archers of Crecy and Agincourt who fought in 1914 beside the hard-pressed ranks of England's glorious "Old Contemptibles."

Less intense than Mr. Machen in delineating the extremes of stark fear, yet infinitely more closely wedded to the idea of an unreal world constantly pressing upon ours is the inspired and prolific Algernon Blackwood, amidst whose voluminous and uneven work may be found some of the finest spectral literature of this or any age. Of the quality of Mr. Blackwood's genius there can be no dispute; for no one has even approached the skill, seriousness, and minute fidelity with which he records the overtones of strangeness in ordinary things and experiences, or the preternatural insight with which he builds up detail by detail the complete sensations and perceptions leading from reality into supernormal life or vision. Without notable command of the poetic witchery of mere words, he is the one absolute and unquestioned master of weird atmosphere; and can evoke what amounts almost to a story from a simple fragment of humourless psychological description. Above all others he understands how fully some sensitive minds dwell forever on the borderland of dream, and how relatively slight is the distinction betwixt those images formed from actual objects and those excited by the play of the imagination.

Mr. Blackwood's lesser work is marred by several defects such as ethical didacticism, occasional insipid whimsicality, the flatness of benignant supernaturalism, and a too free use of the trade jargon of modern "occultism." A fault of his more serious efforts is that diffuseness and long-windedness which results from an excessively elaborate attempt, under the handicap of a somewhat bald and journalistic style devoid of intrinsic magic, colour, and vitality, to visualise precise sensations and nuances of uncanny suggestion. But in spite of all this, the major products of Mr. Blackwood attain a genuinely classic level, and evoke as does nothing else in literature in awed convinced sense of the imminence of strange spiritual spheres of entities.

The well-nigh endless array of Mr. Blackwood's fiction includes both novels and shorter tales, the latter sometimes independent and sometimes arrayed in series. Foremost of all must be reckoned *The Willows*, in which the nameless presences on a desolate Danube island are horribly felt and recognised by a pair of idle voyagers. Here art and restraint in narrative reach their very highest development, and an impression of lasting poignancy is produced without a single strained passage or a single false note. Another amazingly potent though less artistically finished tale is *The Wendigo*, where we are confronted by horrible evidences of a vast forest dæmon about which North Woods lumbermen whisper at evening. The manner in which certain footprints tell certain unbelievable things is really a marked triumph in craftsmanship. In *An Episode in a Lodging House* we behold frightful presences summoned out of black space by a sorcerer, and *The Listener* tells of the awful psychic residuum creeping about an old house where a leper died. In the volume titled *Incredible Adventures* occur some of the finest tales which the author has yet produced, leading the fancy to wild rites on nocturnal hills, to secret and terrible aspects lurking behind stolid scenes, and to unimaginable vaults of mystery below the sands and pyramids of Egypt; all with a serious finesse and delicacy that convince where a cruder or lighter treatment would merely amuse. Some of these accounts are hardly stories at all, but rather studies in elusive impressions and half-remembered snatches of dream. Plot is everywhere negligible, and atmosphere reigns untrammelled.

John Silence — Physician Extraordinary is a book of five related tales, through which a single character runs his triumphant course. Marred only by traces of the popular and conventional detective-story atmosphere — for Dr. Silence is one of those benevolent geniuses who employ their remarkable powers to aid worthy fellow-men in difficulty — these narratives contain some of the author's best work, and produce an illusion at once emphatic and lasting. The opening tale, *A Psychical Invasion*, relates what befell a sensitive author in a house once the scene of dark deeds, and how a legion of fiends was exorcised. *Ancient Sorceries*, perhaps the finest tale in the book, gives an almost hypnotically vivid account of an old French town where once the unholy Sabbath was kept by all the people in the form of cats. In *The Nemesis of Fire* a hideous elemental is evoked by new-spilt blood, whilst *Secret Worship* tells of a German school where

Satanism held sway, and where long afterward an evil aura remained. *The Camp of the Dog* is a werewolf tale, but is weakened by moralisation and professional "occultism."

Too subtle, perhaps, for definite classification as horror-tales, yet possibly more truly artistic in an absolute sense, are such delicate phantasies as *Jimbo* or *The Centaur*. Mr. Blackwood achieves in these novels a close and palpitant approach to the inmost substance of dream, and works enormous havoc with the conventional barriers between reality and imagination.

Unexcelled in the sorcery of crystalline singing prose, and supreme in the creation of a gorgeous and languorous world of iridescently exotic vision, is Edward John Moreton Drax Plunkett, Eighteenth Baron Dunsany, whose tales and short plays form an almost unique element in our literature. Inventor of a new mythology and weaver of surprising folk-lore, Lord Dunsany stands dedicated to a strange world of fantastic beauty, and pledged to eternal warfare against the coarseness and ugliness of diurnal reality. His point of view is the most truly cosmic of any held in the literature of any period. As sensitive as Poe to dramatic values and the significance of isolated words and details, and far better equipped rhetorically through a simple lyric style based on the prose of the King James Bible, this author draws with tremendous effectiveness on nearly every body of myth and legend within the circle of European culture; producing a composite or eclectic cycle of phantasy in which Eastern colour, Hellenic form, Teutonic sombreness and Celtic wistfulness are so superbly blended that each sustains and supplements the rest without sacrifice or perfect congruity and homogeneity. In most cases Dunsany's lands are fabulous —

"beyond the East," or "at the edge of the world." His system of original personal and place names, with roots drawn from classical, Oriental, and other sources, is a marvel of versatile inventiveness and poetic discrimination; as one may see from such specimens as "Argimenes," "Beth-moora," "Poltarnees," "Camorak," "Iluriel," or "Sardath-rion."

Beauty rather than terror is the keynote of Dunsany's work. He loves the vivid green of jade and of copper domes, and the delicate flush of sunset on the ivory minarets of impossible dream-cities. Humour and irony, too, are often present to impart a gentle cynicism and modify what might otherwise possess a naïve intensity. Nevertheless, as is inevitable in a master of triumphant unreality, there are occasional touches of cosmic fright which come well within the authentic tradition. Dunsany loves to hint slyly and adroitly of monstrous things and incredible dooms, as one hints in a fairy tale. In *The Book of Wonder* we read of Hlo-Hlo, the gigantic spider-idol which does not always stay at home; of what the Sphinx feared in the forest; of Slith, the thief who jumps over the edge of the world after seeing a certain light lit and knowing who lit it; of the anthropophagous Gib-belins, who inhabit an evil tower and guard a treasure; of the Gnoles, who live in the forest and from whom it is not well to steal; of the City of Never, and the eyes that watch in the Under Pits; and of kindred things of darkness. *A Dreamer's Tales* tells of the mystery that sent forth all men from Bethmoora in the desert; of the vast gate of Perdon-daris, that was carved from a single piece of ivory; and of the voyage of poor old Bill, whose captain cursed the crew and paid calls on nasty-looking isles new-risen from the sea, with low thatched cottages having evil, obscure windows.

Many of Dunsany's short plays are replete with spectral fear. In *The Gods of the Mountain* seven beggars impersonate the seven green idols on a distant hill, and enjoy ease and honour in a city of worshippers until they hear that the real idols are missing from their wonted seats. A very ungainly sight in the dusk is reported to them — "rock should not walk in the evening" — and at last, as they sit awaiting the arrival of a troop of dancers, they note that the approaching footsteps are heavier than those of good dancers ought to be. Then things ensue, and in the end the presumptuous blasphemers are turned to green jade statues by the very walking statues whose sanctity they outraged. But mere plot is the very least merit of this marvellously effective play. The incidents and developments are those of a supreme master, so that the whole forms one of the most important contributions of the present age not only to drama, but to literature in general. *A Night at an Inn* tells of four thieves who have stolen the emerald eye of Klesh, a monstrous Hindoo god. They lure to their room and succeed in slaying the three priestly avengers who are on their track, but in the night Klesh comes gropingly for his eye; and having gained it and departed, calls each of the despoilers out into the darkness for an unnamed punishment. In *The Laughter of the Gods* there is a doomed city at the jungle's edge, and a ghostly lutanist heard only by those about to die (*cf.* Alice's spectral harpsichord in Hawthorne's *House of the Seven Gables*); whilst *The Queen's Enemies* retells the anecdote of Herodotus in which a vengeful princess invites her foes to a subterranean banquet and lets in the Nile to drown them. But no amount of mere description can convey more than a fraction of Lord Dunsany's pervasive charm. His prismatic cities and unheard of rites are touched with a sureness which only mastery can engender, and we thrill with a sense of actual participation in his secret mysteries. To the truly imaginative he is a talisman and a key unlocking rich storehouses of dream and fragmentary memory; so that we may think of him not only as a poet, but as one who makes each reader a poet as well.

At the opposite pole of genius from Lord Dunsany, and gifted with an almost diabolic power of calling horror by gentle steps from the midst of prosaic daily life, is the scholarly Montague Rhodes James, Provost of Eton College, antiquary of note, and recognized authority on mediæval manuscripts and cathedral history. Dr. James, long fond of telling spectral tales at Christmastide, has become by slow degrees a literary weird fictionist of the very first rank; and has developed a distinctive style and method likely to serve as models for an enduring line of disciples.

The art of Dr. James is by no means haphazard, and in the preface to one of his collections he has formulated three very sound rules for macabre composition. A ghost story, he believes, should have a familiar setting in the modern period, in order to approach closely the reader's sphere of experience. Its spectral phenomena, moreover, should be malevolent rather than beneficent; since fear is the emotion primarily to be excited. And finally, the technical patois of "occultism" or pseudo-science ought carefully to be avoided; lest the charm of casual verisimilitude be smothered in unconvincing pedantry.

Dr. James, practicing what he preaches, approaches his themes in a light and often conversational way. Creating the illusion of every-day events, he introduces his abnormal phenomena cautiously and gradually, relieved at every turn by touches of homely and prosaic detail, and sometimes spiced with a snatch or two of antiquarian scholarship. Conscious of the close relation between present weirdness and accumulated tradition, he generally provides remote historical antecedents for his incidents; thus being able to utilise very aptly his exhaustive knowledge of the past, and his ready and convincing command of archaic diction and colouring. A favourite scene for a James tale is some centuried cathedral, which the author can describe with all the familiar minuteness of a specialist in that field.

Sly humourous vignettes and bits of lifelike genre portraiture and characterisation are often to be found in Dr. James's narratives, and serve in his skilled hands to augment the general effect rather than to spoil it, as the same qualities would tend to do with a lesser craftsman. In inventing a new type of ghost, he has departed considerably from the conventional Gothic tradition; for where the older stock ghosts were pale and stately, and apprehended chiefly through the sense of sight, the average James ghost is lean, dwarfish, and hairy — a sluggish, hellish night-abomination midway betwixt beast and man — and usually touched before it is seen. Sometimes the spectre is of still more eccentric composition: a roll of flannel with spidery eyes, or an invisible entity which moulds itself in bedding and shows a face of crumpled linen. Dr. James has, it is clear, an intelligent and scientific knowledge of human nerves and feelings; and knows just how to apportion statement, imagery, and subtle suggestions in order to secure the best results with his readers. He is an artist in incident and arrangement rather than in atmosphere, and reaches the emotions more often through the intellect than directly. This method, of course, with its occasional absences of sharp climax, has its drawbacks as well as its advantages; and many will miss the thorough atmospheric tension which writers like Machen are careful to build up with words and scenes. But only a few of the tales are open to the charge of tameness. Generally the laconic unfolding of abnormal events in adroit order is amply sufficient to produce the desired effect of cumulative horror.

The short stories of Dr. James are contained in four small collections, entitled respectively *Ghost Stories of an Antiquary, More Ghost Stories of an Antiquary, A Thin Ghost and Others*, and *A Warning to the Curious*. There is also a delightful juvenile phantasy, *The Five Jars*, which has its spectral adumbrations. Amidst this wealth of material it is hard to select a favourite or especially typical tale, though each reader will no doubt have such preferences as his temperament may determine.

Count Magnus is assuredly one of the best, forming as it does a veritable Golconda of suspense and suggestion. Mr. Wraxall is an English traveller of the middle nineteenth century, sojourning in Sweden to secure material for a book. Becoming interested in the ancient family of De La Gardie, near the village of Raback, he studies its records; and finds particular fascination in the builder of the existing Manor-house, one Count Magnus, of whom strange and terrible things are whispered. The Count, who flourished early in the seventeenth century, was a stern landlord, and famous for his severity toward poachers and delinquent tenants. His cruel punishments were bywords, and there were dark rumours of influences which even survived his interment in the great mausoleum he built near the church — as in the case of the two peasants who hunted on his preserves one night a century after his death. There were hideous screams in the woods, and near the tomb of Count Magnus an unnatural laugh and the clang of a great door. Next morning the priest found the two men; one a maniac, and the other dead, with the flesh of his face sucked from the bones.

Mr. Wraxall hears all these tales, and stumbles on more guarded references to a Black Pilgrimage once taken by the Count, a pilgrimage to Chorazin in Palestine, one of the cities denounced by Our Lord in the Scriptures, and in which old priests say that Antichrist is to be born. No one dares to hint just what that Black Pilgrimage was, or what strange being or thing the Count brought back as a companion. Meanwhile Mr. Wraxall is increasingly anxious to explore the mausoleum of Count Magnus, and finally secures permission to do so, in the company of a deacon. He finds several monuments and three copper sarcophagi, one of which is the Count's. Round the edge of this latter are several bands of engraved scenes, including a singular and hideous delineation of a pursuit — the pursuit of a frantic man through a forest by a squat muffled figure with a devil-fish's tentacle, directed by a tall cloaked man on a neighbouring hillock. The sarcophagus has three massive steel padlocks, one of which is lying open on the floor, reminding the traveller of a metallic clash he heard the day before when passing the mausoleum and wishing idly that he might see Count Magnus.

His fascination augmented, and the key being accessible, Mr. Wraxall pays the mausoleum a second and solitary visit and finds another padlock unfastened. The next day, his last in Raback, he again goes alone to bid the long-dead Count farewell. Once more queerly impelled to utter a whimsical wish for a meeting with the buried nobleman, he now sees to his disquiet that only one of the padlocks remains on the great sarcophagus. Even as he looks, that last lock drops noisily to the floor, and there comes a sound as of creaking hinges. Then the monstrous lid appears very slowly to rise, and Mr. Wraxall flees in panic fear without refastening the door of the mausoleum.

During his return to England the traveller feels a curious uneasiness about his fellow-passengers on the canal-boat which he employs for the earlier stages. Cloaked figures make him nervous, and he has a sense of being watched and followed. Of twenty-eight persons whom he counts, only twenty-six appear at meals; and the missing two are always a tall cloaked man and a shorter muffled figure. Completing his water travel at Harwich, Mr. Wraxall takes frankly to flight in a closed carriage, but sees two cloaked figures at a crossroad. Finally he lodges at a small house in a village and spends the time making frantic notes. On the second morning he is found dead, and during the inquest seven jurors faint at sight of the body. The house where he stayed is never again inhabited, and upon its demolition half a century later his manuscript is discovered in a forgotten cupboard.

In *The Treasure of Abbot Thomas* a British antiquary unriddles a cipher on some Renaissance painted windows, and thereby discovers a centuried hoard of gold in a niche halfway down a well in the courtyard of a German abbey. But the crafty depositor had set a guardian over that treasure, and something in the black well twines its arms around the searcher's neck in such a manner that the quest is abandoned, and a clergyman sent for. Each night after that the discoverer feels a stealthy presence and detects a horrible odour of mould outside the door of his hotel room, till finally the clergyman makes a daylight replacement of the stone at the mouth of the treasure-vault in the well — out of which something had come in the dark to avenge the disturbing of old Abbot Thomas's gold. As he completes his work the cleric observes a curious toad-like carving on the ancient well-head, with the Latin motto "*Depositum custodi* — keep that which is committed to thee."

Other notable James tales are *The Stalls of Barchester Cathedral*, in which a grotesque carving comes curiously to life to avenge the secret and subtle murder of an old Dean by his ambitious successor; *Oh, Whistle, and I'll Come to You*, which tells of the horror summoned by a strange metal whistle found in a mediæval church ruin; and *An Episode of Cathedral History*, where the dismantling of a pulpit uncovers an archaic tomb whose lurking dæmon spreads panic and pestilence. Dr. James, for all his light touch, evokes fright and hideousness in their most shocking form, and will certainly stand as one of the few really creative masters in his darksome province.

For those who relish speculation regarding the future, the tale of supernatural horror provides an interesting field. Combated by a mounting wave of plodding realism, cynical flippancy, and sophisticated disillusionment, it is yet encouraged by a parallel tide of growing mysticism, as developed both through the fatigued reaction of "occultists" and religious fundamentalists against materialistic discovery and through the stimulation of wonder and fancy by such enlarged vistas and broken barriers as modern science has given us with its intra-atomic chemistry, advancing astrophysics, doctrines of relativity, and probings into biology and human thought. At the present moment the favouring forces would appear to have somewhat of an advantage; since there is unquestionably more cordiality shown toward weird writings than when, thirty years ago, the best of Arthur Machen's work fell on the stony ground of the smart and cocksure 'nineties. Ambrose Bierce, almost unknown in his own time, has now reached something like general recognition.

Startling mutations, however, are not to be looked for in either direction. In any case an approximate balance of tendencies will continue to exist; and while we may justly expect a further subtilisation of technique, we have no reason to think that the general position of the spectral in literature will be altered. It is a narrow though essential branch of human expression, and will chiefly appeal as always to a limited audience with keen special sensibilities. Whatever universal masterpiece of tomorrow may be wrought from phantasm or terror will owe its acceptance rather to a supreme workmanship than to a sympathetic theme. Yet who shall declare the dark theme a positive handicap? Radiant with beauty, the Cup of the Ptolemies was carven of onyx.

NOTES ON WRITING
WEIRD FICTION

My reason for writing stories is to give myself the satisfaction of visualising more clearly and detailedly and stably the vague, elusive, fragmentary impressions of wonder, beauty, and adventurous expectancy which are conveyed to me by certain sights (scenic, architectural, atmospheric, etc.), ideas, occurrences, and images encountered in art and literature. I choose weird stories because they suit my inclination best — one of my strongest and most persistent wishes being to achieve, momentarily, the illusion of some strange suspension or violation of the galling limitations of time, space, and natural law which forever imprison us and frustrate our curiosity about the infinite cosmic spaces beyond the radius of our sight and analysis. These stories frequently emphasise the element of horror because fear is our deepest and strongest emotion, and the one which best lends itself to the creation of Nature-defying illusions. Horror and the unknown or the strange are always closely connected, so that it is hard to create a convincing picture of shattered natural law or cosmic alienage or "outsideness" without laying stress on the emotion of fear. The reason why *time* plays a great part in so many of my tales is that this element looms up in my mind as the most profoundly dramatic and grimly terrible thing in the universe. *Conflict with time* seems to me the most potent and fruitful theme in all human expression.

While my chosen form of story-writing is obviously a special and perhaps a narrow one, it is none the less a persistent and permanent type of expression, as old as literature itself. There will always be a certain small percentage of persons who feel a burning curiosity about unknown outer space, and a burning desire to escape from the prison-house of the known and the real into those enchanted lands of incredible adventure and infinite possibilities which dreams open up to us, and which things like deep woods, fantastic urban towers, and flaming sunsets momentarily suggest. These persons include great authors as well as insignificant amateurs like myself — Dunsany, Poe, Arthur Machen, M. R. James, Algernon Blackwood, and Walter de la Mare being typical masters in this field.

As to how I write a story — there is no one way. Each one of my tales has a different history. Once or twice I have literally written out a dream; but usually I start with a mood or idea or image which I wish to express, and revolve it in my mind until I can think of a good way of embodying it in some chain of dramatic occurrences capable of being recorded in concrete terms. I tend to run through a mental list of the basic conditions or situations best adapted to such a mood or idea or image, and then begin to speculate on logical and naturally motivated explanations of the given mood or idea or image in terms of the basic condition or situation chosen.

The actual process of writing is of course as varied as the choice of theme and initial conception; but if the history of all my tales were analysed, it is just possible that the following set of rules might be deduced from the *average* procedure:

Prepare a synopsis or scenario of events in the order of their absolute *occurrence* — *not* the order of their narration. Describe with enough fulness to cover all vital points and motivate all incidents planned. Details, comments, and estimates of consequences are sometimes desirable in this temporary framework.

Prepare a second synopsis or scenario of events — this one in order of *narration* (not actual occurrence), with ample fulness and detail, and with notes as to changing perspective, stresses, and climax. Change the original synopsis to fit if such a change will increase the dramatic force or general effectiveness of the story. Interpolate or delete incidents at will — never being bound by the original conception even if the ultimate result be a tale wholly different from that first planned. Let additions and alterations be made whenever suggested by anything in the formulating process.

Write out the story — rapidly, fluently, and not too critically — following the *second* or narrative-order synopsis. Change incidents and plot whenever the developing process seems to suggest such change, never being bound by any previous design. If the development suddenly reveals new opportunities for dramatic effect or vivid story telling, add whatever is thought advantageous — going back and reconciling the early parts to the new plan. Insert and delete whole sections if necessary or desirable, trying different beginnings and endings until the best arrangement is found.

But be sure that all references throughout the story are thoroughly reconciled with the final design. Remove all possible superfluities — words, sentences, paragraphs, or whole episodes or elements — observing the usual precautions about the reconciling of all references.

Revise the entire text, paying attention to vocabulary, syntax, rhythm of prose, proportioning of parts, niceties of tone, grace and convincingness of transitions (scene to scene, slow and detailed action to rapid and sketchy time-covering action and vice versa... etc., etc., etc.), effectiveness of beginning, ending, climaxes, etc., dramatic suspense and interest, plausibility and atmosphere, and various other elements.

Prepare a neatly typed copy — not hesitating to add final revisory touches where they seem in order.

The first of these stages is often purely a mental one — a set of conditions and happenings being worked out in my head, and never set down until I am ready to prepare a detailed synopsis of events in order of narration. Then, too, I sometimes begin even the actual writing before I know how I shall develop the idea — this beginning forming a problem to be motivated and exploited.

There are, I think, four distinct types of weird story; one expressing a *mood or feeling,* another expressing a *pictorial conception,* a third expressing a *general situation, condition, legend or intellectual conception,* and a fourth explaining a *definite tableau or specific dramatic situation or climax.* In another way, weird tales may be grouped into two rough categories — those in which the marvel or horror concerns some *condition* or *phenomenon,* and those in which it concerns some *action of persons* in connexion with a bizarre condition or phenomenon.

Each weird story — to speak more particularly of the horror type — seems to involve five definite elements:

(a) some basic, underlying horror or abnormality — condition, entity, etc. —,
(b) the general effects or bearings of the horror,
(c) the mode of manifestation — object embodying the horror and phenomena observed —,
(d) the types of fear-reaction pertaining to the horror, and
(e) the specific effects of the horror in relation to the given set of conditions.

In writing a weird story I always try very carefully to achieve the right mood and atmosphere, and place the emphasis where it belongs. One cannot, except in immature pulp charlatan-fiction, present an account of impossible, improbable, or inconceivable phenomena as a commonplace narrative of objective acts and conventional emotions. Inconceivable events and conditions have a special handicap to overcome, and this can be accomplished only through the maintenance of a careful realism in every phase of the story *except* that touching on the one given marvel. This marvel must be treated very impressively and deliberately — with a careful emotional "build-up" — else it will seem flat and unconvincing. Being the principal thing in the story, its mere existence should overshadow the characters and events. But the characters and events must be consistent and natural except where they touch the single marvel. In relation to the central wonder, the characters should shew the same overwhelming emotion which similar characters would shew toward such a wonder in real life. Never have a wonder taken for granted. Even when the characters are supposed to be accustomed to the wonder I try to weave an air of awe and impressiveness corresponding to what the reader should feel. A casual style ruins any serious fantasy.

Atmosphere, not action, is the great desideratum of weird fiction. Indeed, all that a wonder story can ever be is *a vivid picture of a certain type of human mood.* The moment it tries to be anything else it becomes cheap, puerile, and unconvincing. Prime emphasis should be given to *subtle* suggestion — imperceptible hints and touches of selective associative detail which express shadings of moods and build up a vague illusion of the strange reality of the unreal. Avoid bald catalogues of incredible happenings which can have no substance or meaning apart from a sustaining cloud of colour and symbolism.

These are the rules or standards which I have followed — consciously or unconsciously — ever since I first attempted the serious writing of fantasy. That my results are successful may well be disputed — but I feel at least sure that, had I ignored the considerations mentioned in the last few paragraphs, they would have been much worse than they are.

NOTES ON WRITING
INTERPLANETARY FICTION

DESPITE the current flood of stories dealing with other worlds and universes, and with intrepid flights to and from them through cosmic space, it is probably no exaggeration to say that not more than a half-dozen of these things, including the novels of H. G. Wells, have even the slightest shadow of a claim to artistic seriousness or literary rank. Insincerity, conventionality, triteness, artificiality, false emotion, and puerile extravagance reign triumphant throughout this overcrowded genre, so that none but its rarest products can possibly claim a truly adult status. And the spectacle of such persistent hollowness has led many to ask whether, indeed, any fabric of real literature can ever grow out of the given subject-matter.

The present commentator does not believe that the idea of space-travel and other worlds is inherently unsuited to literary use. It is, rather, his opinion that the omnipresent cheapening and misuse of that idea is the result of a widespread misconception; a misconception which extends to other departments of weird and science fiction as well. This fallacy is the notion that any account of impossible, improb-

119

able, or inconceivable phenomena can be successfully presented as a commonplace narrative of objective acts and conventional emotions in the ordinary tone and manner of popular romance. Such a presentation will often "get by" with immature readers, but it will never approach even remotely the field of æsthetic merit.

Inconceivable events and conditions form a class apart from all other story elements, and cannot be made convincing by any mere process of casual narration. They have the handicap of incredibility to overcome; and this can be accomplished only through a careful realism in every *other* phase of the story, plus a gradual atmospheric or emotional building-up of the utmost subtlety. The emphasis, too, must be kept right—hovering always over *the wonder of the central abnormality itself*. It must be remembered that any violation of what we know as natural law is *in itself* a far more tremendous thing than any other event or feeling which could possibly affect a human being. Therefore in a story dealing with such a thing we cannot expect to create any sense of life or illusion of reality if we treat the wonder casually and have the characters moving about under ordinary motivations. The characters, though they must be natural, should be subordinated to the central marvel around which they are grouped. The true "hero" of a marvel tale is not any human being, but simply a *set of phenomena*.

Over and above everything else should tower the stark, outrageous monstrousness of the one chosen departure from Nature. The characters should react to it as real people would react to such a thing if it were suddenly to confront them in daily life; displaying the almost soul-shattering amazement which anyone would naturally display instead of the mild, tame, quickly-passed-over emotions prescribed by cheap popular convention. Even when the wonder is one to which the characters are assumed to be used, the sense of awe, marvel, and strangeness which the reader would feel in the presence of such a thing must somehow be suggested by the author. When an account of a marvellous trip is presented without the colouring of appropriate emotion, we never feel the least degree of vividness in it. We do not get the spine-tickling illusion that such a thing might possibly have happened, but merely feel that somebody has uttered some extravagant words. In general, we should forget all about the popular hack conventions of cheap writing and try to make our story a perfect slice of actual life except where the one chosen marvel is concerned. We should work as if we were staging a hoax and trying to get our extravagant lie accepted as literal truth.

Atmosphere, not action, is the thing to cultivate in the wonder story. We cannot put stress on the bare events, since the unnatural extravagance of these events makes them sound hollow and absurd when thrown into too-high relief. Such events, even when theoretically possible or conceivable in the future, have no counterpart or basis in existing life and human experience, hence can never form the groundwork of an adult tale. All that a marvel story can ever be, in a serious way, is *a vivid picture of a certain type of human mood*. The moment it tries to be anything else it becomes cheap, puerile, and unconvincing. Therefore, a fantastic author should see that his prime emphasis goes into subtle suggestion—the imperceptible hints and touches of selective and associative detail which express shadings of moods and build up a vague illusion of the strange reality of the unreal—instead of into bald catalogues of incredible happenings which can have no substance or meaning apart from a sustaining cloud of colour and mood-symbolism. A serious adult story must be true to something in life. Since marvel tales cannot be true to the *events* of life, they must shift their emphasis toward something to which they *can* be true; namely, certain wistful or restless *moods* of the human spirit, wherein it seeks to weave gossamer ladders of escape from the galling tyranny of time, space, and natural law.

And how are these general principles of adult wonder fiction to be applied to the interplanetary tale in particular? That they *can* be applied, we have no reason to doubt; the important factors being here, as elsewhere, an adequate sense of wonder, adequate emotions in the characters, realism in the setting and supplementary incidents, care in the choice of significant detail, and a studious avoidance of the hackneyed artificial characters and stupid conventional events and situations which at once destroy a story's vitality by proclaiming it a product of weary mass mechanics. It is an ironic truth that no artistic story of this kind, honestly, sincerely, and unconventionally written, would be likely to have any chance of acceptance among professional editors of the common pulp school. This, however, will not influence the really determined artist bent on creating something of mature worth. Better to write honestly for a non-remunerative magazine than to concoct worthless tinsel and be paid for it. Some day, perhaps, the conventions of editors will be less flagrantly absurd in their anti-artistic rigidity. The events of an interplanetary story—aside from such tales as involve sheer poetic fantasy—are best laid in the present, or represented as having occurred secretly or prehistorically in the past. The future is a ticklish period to deal with; since it is virtually impossible to escape grotesqueness and absurdity in depicting its mode of life, while there is always an immense emotional loss in representing characters as familiar with the marvels depicted. The characters of a story are essentially projections of ourselves; and unless they can share our own ignorance and wonder concerning what occurs, there is an inevitable handicap. This is not to say that tales of the future cannot be artistic, but merely that it is harder to make them so.

A good interplanetary story must have realistic human characters; not the stock scientists, villainous assistants, invincible heroes, and lovely scientists-daughter heroines of the usual trash of this sort. Indeed, there is no reason why there should be any "villain", "hero", or "heroine" at all. These artificial character-types belong wholly to artificial plot-forms, and have no place in serious fiction of any kind. The function of the story is to express a certain human mood of wonder and liberation, and any tawdry dragging-in of dime-novel theatricalism is both out of place and injurious. No stock romance is wanted. We must select only such characters (not necessarily stalwart or picturesque characters) as would naturally be involved in the events to be depicted, and they must behave exactly as real persons would behave if confronted with the given marvels. The tone of the whole thing must be realism, not romance.

The crucial and delicate matter of getting the characters off the earth must be very carefully managed. Indeed, it probably forms the greatest single problem of the story. The departure must be plausibly accounted for and impressively described. If the period is not prehistoric, it is better to have the means of departure a secret invention. The characters must react to this invention with a proper sense of utter, almost paralysing wonder, avoiding the cheap fictional tendency of having such things half taken for granted. To avoid errors in complex problems of physics, it is well not to attempt too much detail in describing the invention.

Scarcely less delicate is the problem of describing the voyage through space and the landing on another world. Here we must lay primary stress on the stupendous emotions—the unconquerable sense of astonishment—felt by the voyagers as they realise they are *actually off their native earth*, in cosmic gulfs or on an alien world. Needless to say, a strict following of scientific fact in representing the mechanical, astronomical, and other aspects of the trip is absolutely essential. Not all readers are ignorant of the sciences, and a flagrant contravention of truth ruins a tale for anyone able to detect it.

Equal scientific care must be given to our representation of events on the alien planet. Everything must be in strict accord with the known or assumed nature of the orb in question—surface gravity, axial inclination, length of day and year, aspect of sky, etc.—and the atmosphere must be built up with significant details conducing to verisimilitude and realism. Hoary stock devices connected with the reception of the voyagers by the planet's inhabitants ought to be ruled rigidly out. Thus we should have no over-facile language-learning; no telepathic communication; no worship of the travellers as deities; no participation in the affairs of pseudo-human kingdoms, or in conventional wars between factions of inhabitants; no weddings with beautiful anthropomorphic princesses; no stereotyped Armageddons with ray-guns and space-ships; no court intrigues and jealous magicians; no peril from hairy ape-men of the polar caps; and so on, and so on. Social and political satire is always undesirable, since such intellectual and ulterior objects detract from the story's power as a crystallisation of a mood. What must always be present in superlative degree is a deep, pervasive sense of *strangeness*—the utter, incomprehensible *strangeness* of a world holding nothing in common with ours.

It is not necessary that the alien planet be inhabited—or inhabited at the period of the voyage—at all. If it is, the denizens must be definitely non-human in aspect, mentality, emotions, and nomenclature, unless they are assumed to be descendants of a prehistoric colonising expedition from our earth. The human-like aspect, psychology, and proper names commonly attributed to other-planetarians by the bulk of cheap authors is at once hilarious and pathetic. Another absurd habit of conventional hacks is having the major denizens of other planets always more advanced scientifically and mechanically than ourselves; always indulging in spectacular rites against a background of cubistic temples and palaces, and always menaced by some monstrous and dramatic peril. This kind of pap should be replaced by an adult realism, with the races of other-planetarians represented, according to the artistic demands of each separate case, as in every stage of development — sometimes high, sometimes low, and sometimes unpicturesquely middling. Royal and religious pageantry should not be conventionally overemphasised; indeed, it is not at all likely that more than a fraction of the exotic races would have lit upon the especial folk-customs of royalty and religion. It must be remembered that non-human beings would be wholly apart from human motives and perspectives.

But the real nucleus of the story ought to be something far removed from the specific aspect and customs of any hypothetical outside race—ought, indeed, to be nothing less than the *simple sensation of wonder at being off the earth*. Interest had better be sustained through accounts of bizarre and un-terrestrial natural conditions, rather than through any artificially dramatic actions of the characters, either human or exotic. Adventures may well be introduced, but they should be properly subordinated to realism —made inevitable outgrowths of the conditions instead of synthetic thrills concocted for their own sake.

The climax and ending must be managed very carefully to avoid extravagance or artificiality. It is preferable, in the interest of convincingness, to represent the fact of the voyage as remaining hidden from the public—or to have the voyage a prehistoric affair, forgotten by mankind and with its rediscovery remaining a secret. The idea of any general revelation implying a widespread change in human thoughts, history, or orientation tends to contradict surrounding events and clash with actual future probabilities too radically to give the reader a sense of naturalness. It is far more potent not to make the truth of the story dependent on any condition visibly contradicting what we know—for the reader may pleasantly toy with the notion that *perhaps* these marvels *may* have happened after all!

Meanwhile the deluge of inept interplanetary tosh continues. Whether a qualitative upturn will ever occur on anything like a large scale, this commentator cannot venture to prophesy; but at any rate, he has had his say regarding what he deems the main aspects of the problem. There are, without doubt, great possibilities in the serious exploitation of the astronomical tale; as a few semi-classics like *The War of the Worlds, Last and First Men, Station X,* "The Red Brain", and Clark Ashton Smith's best work prove. But the pioneers must be prepared to labour without financial return, professional recognition, or the encouragement of a reading majority whose taste has been seriously warped by the rubbish it has devoured. Fortunately sincere artistic creation is its own incentive and reward, so that despite all obstacles we need not despair of the future of a fresh literary form whose present lack of development leaves all the more room for brilliant and fruitful experimentation.

ABOUT THE AUTHOR

Howard Phillips "H. P." Lovecraft (August 20, 1890 – March 15, 1937) was an American author of horror, fantasy and science fiction, especially the subgenre known as weird fiction.

Lovecraft's guiding literary principle was what he termed "cosmicism" or "cosmic horror", the idea that life is incomprehensible to human minds and that the universe is fundamentally alien. Those who genuinely reason, like his protagonists, gamble with sanity. As early as the 1940s, Lovecraft's work had developed a cult following for his Cthulhu Mythos, a series of loosely interconnected fiction featuring a pantheon of humanity-nullifying entities, as well as the Necronomicon, a fictional grimoire of magical rites and forbidden lore. His works were deeply pessimistic and cynical, challenging the values of the Enlightenment, Romanticism, Humanism and Christianity. Lovecraft's protagonists usually achieve the antithesis of traditional gnosis and mysticism by momentarily glimpsing the horror of ultimate reality and the abyss.

Although Lovecraft's readership was limited during his life, his reputation has grown over the decades, and he is now regarded as one of the most influential horror writers of the 20th century. According to Joyce Carol Oates, Lovecraft — as with Edgar Allan Poe in the 19th century — has exerted "an incalculable influence on succeeding generations of writers of horror fiction". Stephen King called Lovecraft "the twentieth century's greatest practitioner of the classic horror tale." King has even made it clear in his semi-autobiographical non-fiction book *Danse Macabre* that Lovecraft was responsible for his own fascination with horror and the macabre, and was the single largest figure to influence his fiction writing.

Lovecraft's themes and ideas have had a profound effect on culture and literature in general, and have embedded themselves into the foundation that is used for horror associated with the strange.